Becoming Missional

Becoming Missional

*Denominations and New Church Development
in Complex Social Contexts*

DAVID W. BOSHART

WIPF & STOCK · Eugene, Oregon

BECOMING MISSIONAL
Denominations and New Church Development in Complex Social Contexts

Copyright © 2011 David W. Boshart. All rights reserved. Except for brief quotations in critical publications or reviews, no part of this book may be reproduced in any manner without prior written permission from the publisher. Write: Permissions, Wipf and Stock Publishers, 199 W. 8th Ave., Suite 3, Eugene, OR 97401.

Wipf & Stock
An Imprint of Wipf and Stock Publishers
199 W. 8th Ave., Suite 3
Eugene, OR 97401
www.wipfandstock.com

ISBN 13: 978-1-60899-698-8

Manufactured in the U.S.A.

All scripture quotations, unless otherwise indicated, are taken from the Holy Bible, New International Version®, NIV®. Copyright ©1973, 1978, 1984 by Biblica, Inc.™ Used by permission of Zondervan. All rights reserved worldwide.

*Dedicated to my wife, Shana,
who is my partner in all things.*

*And to those heroic leaders
who are the vanguard of the life to come,
who lead the church to dwell
where sin, brokenness, and alienation live,
waiting in hope for redemption.*

Contents

Acknowledgments ix
Introduction xi

PART 1 CONCEPTS 1

1 Organizational Cultural and Change 3

2 Missional Ecclesiology 12

3 Church Planting 23

PART 2 PERSPECTIVES 35

4 Denominational and Conference Leaders 37

5 Iglesia Menonita 54

6 Community Mennonite Church 66

7 New Covenant Hmong Mennonite Church 82

8 Hospitality House 93

PART 3 CONCLUSIONS 109

9 Cross-Case Analysis 111

10 Findings and Recommendations 133

Afterword 151
Appendix A: Definitions 153
Appendix B: Twelve Indicators of the Missional Church 157
About the Author 158
Bibliography 159

Acknowledgments

THIS PROJECT WOULD NOT have been possible without the strong and caring support of many people in my life. First I would like to thank the members of the West Union Mennonite Church, my church family for the past fourteen years and a faith community that honored me by calling me their pastor. These brothers and sisters have not only supported me in my research but also cheered me on to completion. I am immensely grateful for the gift of a four-month sabbatical to focus on the data collection and writing, free of the responsibilities of church leadership.

I am grateful also to denominational and conference leaders who remain nameless in this document for the sake of confidentiality. They demonstrated transparency and true hospitality in welcoming my probing questions. This I take as their earnest, loving, and courageous desire for deepened understanding about the nature of the church, particularly at this point in their denomination's early formation.

The church planters and those who assist them in developing new congregations opened their world in ways that have profoundly impacted my understanding of the church in mission. These heroic leaders are the most self-conscious vanguard of the reign of God I have ever encountered in the church. Working against all odds, they fearlessly press forward because, as one church planter has said, this work is "good." In hearing their stories and struggles, I alternately found myself moved to tears and to prayer.

I am extremely grateful to the faculty of the Leadership Program at Andrews University who have so graciously guided my journey in the leadership program. Special thanks goes to Erich Baumgartner, my dissertation chair, and Shirley Freed, my methodologist. Erich's consistent affirmation that a way would emerge through the mysteries waiting to be understood enabled me to continue in hope. His awareness of and engagement in mission and leadership development provided the mentoring I needed to do this project at the nexus of theology, organizational development, and grassroots church planting. Shirley's remarkable instincts in conceptualizing how to structure the data analysis was invaluable. Her encouragement to "get writing" was the springboard for progress. I count her a formative mentor in the art of qualitative research.

I am grateful to my good friend and mentor, Alan Kreider, for taking the time out of his own very busy and productive sabbatical to read early drafts of my dissertation that contained concepts in need of significant refinement. Alan's unflagging hospitality, love of the church, commitment to mission, and generosity in guiding the learning of persons like myself makes him, to my mind, "great in the kingdom."

Thanks to Amy Spencer for her insightful skill in moving a rather pedantic manuscript into something readable. It was evident in all her suggestions that this project needed to be about equipping thought leaders for the sake of empowering the church for mission.

Finally, I thank those who live closest to me and who see me in my most honest moments. I am ever-grateful to my wife, Shana, who endures my outloud and uncensored thinking and who helps me translate my random and often scattered ideas into clearer and more coherent expression. And thanks to my children, who believed from the first day that this program was a good thing to do with my time. Thanks be to God.

Introduction

IN THIS FIRST FULL decade of the third millennium, discussions of church planting abound, many of them focusing on how to create churches that are relevant in certain contexts, such as in inner cities or immigrant enclaves or suburbs. Some discussions go a step further, seeking to redefine *church* itself.

To these discussions, I add this book, which is based on a study of churches being planted in Mennonite Church USA, a denomination that has been undergoing systemic change and whose mission paradigms are shifting—but not as smoothly or as quickly as hoped.. In Mennonite Church USA, as in other denominations to varying degrees, tensions reside between the traditional "church with a mission" model and the newer "missional church" paradigm (described more fully in chapter 2). At the same time, Mennonite church planters are attempting to establish new churches in a complex social context of discontinuous change.

Here we will explore the outcome of the doctoral study I conducted in 2008–2009 to describe the processes whereby church planters and those who support them develop a common understanding about the nature of the churches being planted in the midst of changing contexts and ecclesial paradigm shifts. These issues are particularly important to me, having been a pastor in Mennonite Church USA for twenty-four years and now as a newly appointed executive conference minister who gives oversight to the mission of a regional area (or conference) of Mennonite Church USA in the upper Midwest.

In the mid-1990s I was asked to co-mediate an entrenched conflict that had developed in a ten-year-old church plant. I offer the story of this church plant in the hopes that it and other narratives in this book will explore issues with which local, regional, and denominational church leaders struggle as they attempt to plant churches at a time when modern models of mission are quickly losing their relevance and coherence. In the process of exploring these issues, we will attempt to identify new pathways forward so that church leaders at every level can incarnate a winsome witness in social contexts that are increasingly characterized by complexity, paradox, and change.

THE STORY OF A CHURCH PLANT[1]

A retired Mennonite pastor moved to the Midwest in the mid-1980s to be nearer to his adult children. Because he had limited means to support his retirement, he developed a proposal to the regional conference of Mennonite Church USA to plant a church in a small Midwestern city of 30,000 people with no Mennonite church and a depressed economy. This city, located on the Mississippi River, once thrived on an industrial-era economy driven by the river, the railroad, and manufacturing. The city planners struggled to find ways of reviving its economy by focusing on education, health care, and technology. Many of these endeavors had taken the city's focus away from downtown and the river to outlying areas of the city that sprawled inland.

Upon accepting the retired pastor's proposal, the regional conference purchased a large home on a bluff overlooking the Mississippi River to serve as the pastor's residence and first meeting place for the church. The conference also agreed to provide a full subsidy for the pastor's salary, with incremental declines in support over the next five years. Two couples from two different states relocated to become the nucleus for the new Mennonite church.

By the fourth year, the church had become a worshipping body of thirty-five people, but the pastor suffered a severe heart attack and could no longer provide leadership for the group. The conference hired another gifted retired pastor and renewed the salary subsidy, with plans to reduce it over the next five years. The congregation grew to forty-five people and then ebbed and flowed between thirty and forty-five several times. By the fifth year, when the salary subsidy was coming to an end, the pastor, now seventy-two, felt he no longer had the energy to lead the church and moved back to his home community in the Southwest. The church dwindled to between twenty-five and thirty participants.

By this time the conference had invested over 200,000 dollars in this project, and the church was still not self-sustaining. Before provid-

---

1. Names of people, churches, and locations involved in my study have been changed, including within direct quotations.

ing more funding to this effort, conference leaders reevaluated the situation and determined that a new kind of leadership was needed. While the two former pastors had been competent, caring individuals, they had served more as chaplains to the small group than as church planters leading with a strategic initiative to grow a church.

Because the core members of the fledgling church had been working together for more than eight years, the conference encouraged them to develop a search committee to secure new leadership. The candidates whom the conference recommended to the search committee were individuals deemed to be more gifted for church growth than for pastoral care. The conference agreed to renew the five-year salary subsidy yet again and to provide additional training to the new leader at a church planting "boot camp"[2] when the new leader was hired.

Unfortunately, the conference leaders and the core group of the church did not talk explicitly about what each entity was expecting from the new leader. The core members of the new church did not realize that the placement of a leader with a strategic agenda for growth would mean this pastor would have a style quite different from that of previous pastors.

The new pastor was hired and relocated with his family, and was coached by conference leaders and denominational mission staff to make church growth and securing a meeting space that would accommodate more people his first priorities. Unaccustomed to this level of assertiveness from their pastors, the core group of the church began to feel controlled and disempowered. Within two years of the church planter's arrival, accusations of dishonesty and abuses of power began to volley between the church planter and lay leaders. It wasn't long before the core group and the new pastor were at an impasse. The church's corporate life ground to a halt. Conference leaders appointed two seasoned pastors from the area to mediate the conflict.

After several sessions of mediation, it was discovered that the conference leadership, the new pastor, and the congregational core group all had different expectations for the role of the new pastor. It was evident that conference leaders and members of the fledgling church all held various assumptions of what a "real" church would look like. These assumptions included a hope to have a building, a church council, a board

---

2. "Boot camps" refers to short-term, intensive church-planter training programs focused on assessment and strategic planning.

of elders, and other traditional organizational structures that replicated other existing churches. These expectations were almost entirely tacit.

While the core group, conference leaders, and new pastor agreed that growing the church was the goal, the core group was not emotionally prepared to embrace the new leadership paradigm. Members of the core group who had relocated to form the nucleus of this church were unwilling to share power with a leader who challenged their decisions.

As the mediation process proceeded, the pastor and core group became increasingly entrenched in accusations of dishonesty and the abuse of power. The pastor-congregation relationship was terminated. While the congregation continued to meet for another five years, it never recovered a vital community life or robust vision for church growth. The congregation carried a deep pain for its perceived failure, and it was unable to extend trust to succeeding leadership. The church closed in the fall of 2005.

THE STORY BEHIND THE STORY

Leadership expert John Kotter writes, "The direction-setting aspect of leadership does not produce plans, it creates vision and strategies. . . . What's crucial about a vision is not its originality but how well it serves the interest of important constituencies."[3] This introductory story is an example of a vision that was neither original nor did it serve the interest of important constituencies. It illustrates how a lack of common understanding at several levels of leadership can result in the corporate self-destruction of a young church.

Knowing the story behind this story—and behind the four other stories described later in this book—can help us begin to see ways that a church planter and other stakeholders can develop a common understanding about the nature of the churches being planted while relating to their denomination, especially in the midst of complex social contexts and during an ecclesial paradigm shift.

In 2001, two Mennonite denominations merged into one, creating Mennonite Church USA. Five years into the transformation process, the

---

3. Kotter, "What Leaders Really Do," 36.

Executive Board of the new denomination offered a refined statement of the denomination's purpose: "Joining in God's activity in the world, [we] develop and nurture missional Mennonite congregations of many cultures."⁴

While the church's denominational leadership and intelligentsia are increasingly committed to a missional ecclesiology, many in the denomination have not experienced this core identity. Recent Executive Board action communicated this reality to the denominational constituency: "As the Executive Board of Mennonite Church USA, we speak with a single and unified voice declaring that our vision and call to engage in God's purposes in the world is not adequately supported by our present relationships, behaviors and organization."⁵

Those involved in denominational, regional, and church-planting leadership in this denomination are caught in a chaotic environment of systemic change between the traditional Christendom models of mission and the new "missional" paradigm. They are further caught by attempting to plant churches in an increasingly post-Christendom cultural context characterized by discontinuous change. According to missional church consultants Alan Roxburgh and Fred Romanuk, "In a period of discontinuous change, leaders suddenly find that skills and capacities in which they were trained are of little use in addressing a new situation and a new environment."⁶

In the past twenty years, the upper Midwestern conference of Mennonite Church USA invested between 1.5 and 2 million dollars in support of developing churches in communities and among ethnic groups where there were no constituent churches. For this traditionally rural denomination, the paradigm for church planting to urban areas had been largely a matter of collecting the "sons and daughters of Menno lost to the city" than doing evangelism. Their primary concern was to create church homes for "cradle" Mennonites far from their childhood church.

The working paradigm for church planting in Mennonite Church USA in the last half of the twentieth century has been influenced by mainline and other Protestant models. In these models, the conference provides full-time financial support for a church planter for the first two

---

4. Mennonite Church USA Executive Board, *Mennonite Church USA 2020*, par. 2.
5. Houser, "Executive Board to Strengthen," 22.
6. Roxburgh and Romanuk, *Missional Leader*, 59.

years. In subsequent years, the subsidy from the conference declines incrementally until no subsidy is provided by the fifth year. The clear hope of the regional conference is that within five years the church planter and a collected core group will have grown to become a self-supporting congregation.

In spite of investing nearly 2 million dollars in the twenty years prior to 2005, no self-supporting congregations had emerged as a result of the church-planting strategy of the regional conference of Mennonite Church USA in the above story. It became clear to conference leaders that it was past time to stop attempting the same strategy, hoping for different results. Without a coherent conceptual framework (ecclesiology), visions originate and develop in seemingly random ways that result in a diffused organizational culture, structure, process, and strategy. When these elements are not aligned with a coherent conceptual framework, the future of the developing church is in peril from the outset.

In 2005, the conference declared a moratorium on significant financial subsidies to church planters. It has since channeled its funding toward the infrastructure needed to develop a more strategic approach to church planting that reflects a "missional ecclesiology." Missional theology, as an ecclesiology, is a recent theoretical genre whose roots can be traced back to the first third of the twentieth century. It has only begun to be identified as a distinct theological paradigm in the past two decades.

In 2005, the conference asked me to accept a volunteer staff role as conference mission strategist to conduct research to deepen the understanding of the process by which church planters and their respective stakeholders come to a common understanding of their task. As the introductory story illustrates, how these understandings are shared by the partners involved is a fundamental issue for which we need better understanding, skill, capacities, and practices. It is self-evident that church planting is intended to bring joyful witness into the world, not self-destructing pain. May the conclusions we explore in this book create greater understanding of the processes that result in a joyful and coherent witness to the reign of God. But first, let's look at the questions on which my conclusions are based.

THE QUESTIONS AT HAND

The following questions formed my doctoral study and the conclusions we will be exploring:

1. In what ways did the relationships, behaviors, and organization of Mennonite Church USA support or fail to support the development of "missional congregations" within Mennonite Church USA and one Midwest regional conference?

2. What common theological commitments were present in the churches being planted in one regional Midwestern conference of Mennonite Church USA, and how were these developing churches aligned with a missional ecclesiology?

3. With what contextual pressures did church planters and their key stakeholders contend in the process of planting churches?

4. How did church planters understand their primary contributions to developing the churches they are planting?[7]

To answer these questions, I first explored the concept of missional theology as a post-Enlightenment ecclesial paradigm. A missional ecclesiology emphasizes that mission originates in the character and purposes of God rather than in the imagination of the church or of specific leaders. The "sent" nature of the church is emphasized. Rather than being sent to build the church, the church is sent to bear witness and be a sign of hope to a world in desperate need of reconciliation, waiting in hope for redemption.

The answers to these questions are also informed by organizational development theory. Missional theology calls for a high degree of sensitivity to context and organizational culture. "For the Christian worker involved in either local church or mission work, issues of organizational culture should be investigated for implications in the life of their organizations," writes Hans Finzel.[8] The emphasis on contextualization and organizational culture in missional theology begs the questions "How do those involved in planting a church function together and how do they develop common understanding about the nature of the churches

---

7. For definitions of some of the terms used in these questions and other portions of this books, see appendix A.

8. Finzel, *Descriptive Model for Discerning*, n.p.

being planted in complex social contexts while at the same time relating to a denomination undergoing systemic change?"

Little has been written on the process whereby church planters and their key stakeholders develop such common understanding. Most books and articles are written by church planters who have experienced some measure of "success." These authors do not intend to offer their stories as models for replication; however, replication does seem to be the default mode for their readers. Without a clear philosophical framework, it is difficult for church planters and their key stakeholders, as with any organization, to develop common understanding for their task, and that results in a confused strategy.

Other literature on church growth, evangelism, and church planting is entirely theological rather than empirical in nature. Theological arguments are important to shaping the life of the church and testing direction, but when a theological framework is present without empirical research, it is difficult to create useful models.

My study demonstrated that church planting, as a function of the church in mission, is best served by a commonly held theology, a clear ecclesiology, a competent understanding of organizational culture, *and* learning through observation of the interplay of these three. Recently a limited body of literature has begun to emerge that synthesizes a theoretical missional framework with empirical data. But very little literature focuses on the cooperative processes at work in the relationship between church planters and their key stakeholders as they work to develop common understanding about the nature of the churches that are being planted in complex social contexts while relating to a larger denominational system.

A FINAL NOTE

It is important for you to understand my worldview as the researcher. Since my study occurred within the context of the church, I assume the significance of the Christian Scriptures as the church's primary source for developing basic assumptions. This research relies on truth revealed in story. As theologian Harry Huebner writes, "What we say to one another on the way is the medium through which the world becomes the world to us."[9] Related to this assumption is the conviction that the particulars

---

9. Huebner, *Echoes of the Word*, 1.

of stories "exemplify more than they describe directly. In the particular is located a general theme," as stated by educator Elliot Eisner.[10]

My study also assumes that church planting is a positive endeavor. There are many motives for church expansion—some honorable, some deplorable, and infinite gradations between. Church planting, rightly motivated, is a worthwhile task.

Finally, I approached this task with a number of biases. I am a leader in the Mennonite church, a group of denominations that trace their roots to the sixteenth-century Anabaptist movement. The core beliefs of the Mennonite church in an Anabaptist perspective emphasize, among other things, discipleship in the way of Jesus, obedience to Scripture as discerned within the gathered community, and peacemaking.

I want and expect the church to be a creative organism that seeks new and vital expressions. I believe in the church. I believe that the church functions with a specific set of cosmological assumptions that differs from the assumptions within secular institutions. Though variations of worldview abound within the broader Christian church, I believe that the church has a basic and unique understanding of what is really real.

---

10. Eisner, *Enlightened Eye*, 39.

Part 1
Concepts

In the creation of the new denomination, Mennonite Church USA leaders proposed a frame-breaking change in the denomination's self-understanding. The framers of the organizational culture and structure of the new denomination declared missional ecclesiology as its foundational commitment. As one can imagine, when two denominations merge, each entity brings a set of expressed and tacit assumptions to the new body representing a complex range of conscious and unconscious organizational, ecclesiological, and theological issues. To understand these issues, we begin by considering some basic assumptions about organizational culture. Then we explore the history and character of a missional ecclesiology. The final chapter in part 1 identifies some of the key issues facing church planters today.

1

Organizational Culture and Change

According to organizational specialist John Kotter, "Interdependence is a key characteristic of modern organizations." He suggests that because of this interdependence, the change process in organizations poses a special challenge to leaders, for unless those involved in the organization "line up and move together in the same direction, people will tend to fall all over one another."[1] This falling over one another is an apt description of the denominational system and the state of church planting in Mennonite Church USA in its first six years of existence.

Getting people to line up and move in the same direction when trying to create systemic change in an organization begins with culture development. Organizational development specialist Edgar Schein suggests, "*The only thing of real importance that leaders do is to create and manage culture* and that the unique talent of leadership is their ability to work with culture." His definition of culture includes "a pattern of basic assumptions."[2] By basic assumptions, he is speaking about the patterns of assumptions that determine all aspects of the organization, how people are valued, how relationships are managed, and what the organization produces.

According to Schein, a culture develops as a response to the organization's attempt to survive through external adaptation and internal integration. He believes that in order to understand an organization's culture, one needs to discern its underlying assumptions "and to identify the paradigm by which the members of a group think about, feel about, and judge situations and relationships."[3] These basic assumptions are similar to what James Sire posits in his *Naming the Elephant: Worldview*

---

1. Kotter, "What Leaders Really Do," 49.
2. Schein, *Organizational Culture*, 2, 9.
3. Ibid., 111.

as a Concept. While worldview is often an individual's understanding of the nature of reality, organizational culture emerges out of the convergence of all the worldviews represented among the members of an organization.

In a later work, Schein anticipates that the contexts in which organizations exist increasingly reflect the complexities of postmodernity. He no longer speaks of one culture represented in an organization; instead, he identifies three. Figuring out how to get these three cultures in true dialogue with each other is key to organizational learning. He has indicated that religious, educational, social, and governmental organizations conceptualize their core mission in different ways as their basic assumptions interact with their specific social context. The three subcultures present in the case of church planting in this book might be characterized as the denominational system (the executive culture), the conference (the interlocutor culture), the church-planting leaders and key stakeholders (the incarnational culture). The executive function is self-evident as the work of conceptualizing, describing, and managing the culture as a whole. The interlocutor culture interprets the culture to the grass roots but also can provide critical feedback to the executive culture that indicates the point to which the denominational culture is being embodied and where such embodiment is resisted. The third culture is described as "incarnational" in that it is trying to *embody* the basic assumptions articulated by the executive culture and interpreted and tested by the interlocutor culture.

All of these subcultures may have differing perspectives on the task at hand. Schein would suggest that the flow of understanding does not move simply from the executive culture through the interlocutor culture to the incarnational culture. Rather, he says, "To create alignment between these three cultures . . . is not a case of deciding which one has the right point of view, but of creating enough mutual understanding between them to evolve solutions that will be understood and implemented." In the current situation of Mennonite Church USA, as an organizational system, it is apparent that the three subcultures operating in the system had not created enough mutual understanding among them "to evolve solutions that will be understood and implemented."[4]

---

4. Schein, *Three Cultures of Management*, par. 45.

ADAPTING TO EXTERNAL CONTEXT

Another aspect of organizational change is the issue of external adaptation. Michael Tushman, William Newman, and Elaine Romanelli suggest in their 1986 *California Management Review* article, "Convergence and Upheaval," that an organization experiences periods of decline in performance due to changes in the external environment that require systemic change. Sometimes an organization becomes so out of touch with the external environment that small adjustments are not adequate to restore organizational effectiveness. This is reflected in the decline of denominations in increasingly postmodern contexts.

Periods calling for this systemic change are referred to as reorientation, described by leadership specialist Gary Yukl as "a relatively short period of intense activity during which top-level leaders make major changes in the organization's structure, strategy and climate."[5] During periods of reorientation, leaders implement significant changes to respond to a changing environment that threatens the success of the organization.

Through empirical research involving alternating processes of "business process reengineering" and "total quality management," Lee Collins and Frances Hill established that organizational change is characterized by generative learning. Generative learning in organizations is the process of becoming actively engaged with a situation for the purposes of developing personal and meaningful understanding of how an organization might optimally relate to its context. Generative learning in organizations is distinguished from adaptive learning that seeks to merely solve problems so the organization can continue on course. Generative learning helps organizations develop the ability "to create the results they truly desire."[6] The goal is to establish total flexibility across the organization in terms of structure, leadership, and intra- and inter-organizational relationships.

The formational documents of Mennonite Church USA seemed to be reaching for total flexibility across the organization. Schein suggests that generative learning, though potentially transformative, is not a natural process. Deciding to expand the capacity for creating a new future does not make it happen. As he writes, "Most generative learn-

---

5. Yukl, *Leadership in Organization*, 358.
6. Collins and Hill, "Descriptive and Analytical Model," 966–83.

ing involves questioning one's basic assumptions, and this is an inherently anxiety provoking process that will be resisted."[7] He describes the four factors of systemic health in an organization that, in large part, will determine the organization's capacity to learn: "(1) a sense of identity, purpose, or mission; (2) a capacity on the part of the system to adapt and maintain itself in the face of internal and external changes; (3) a capacity to perceive and test reality; and (4) some degree of internal integration or alignment of the sub-systems that make up the total system."[8]

It is evident in statements by the Executive Board of Mennonite Church USA that the denomination as a complex system was in the midst of a paradigm shift in the basic assumptions about mission. This shift was an attempt to adapt in the face of internal and external changes. The denomination, by admission of the Executive Board, did not believe it had enough internal organizational alignment among its congregations, denominational agencies, and regional conference structures necessary to realize its mission.[9] The group given the task of developing the organizational culture, strategy, and structure for the new denomination was called the Transformation Team. But it is apparent that naming a process using transformative terminology does not necessarily make it so.

Leaders need to consider carefully how changes affect every level of the organization. They need to lay the groundwork that will cultivate readiness on the part of the organization for transformative rather than merely adaptive changes. Laying the groundwork that prepares organizations for transformative change requires leaders to adequately anticipate layers of resistance. Rather than see resistance as merely an obstacle to progress, strategic leadership will view resistance as an energy in the system that can be leveraged to improve the change process.

Tushman, Newman, and Romanelli suggest that periods of successful reorientation ("that short period of intense activity during which top-level leaders make major changes") will be followed by longer periods of convergence.[10] During convergence, senior leaders make "adjustments" in policy, role clarifications, reallocation of staff and financial resources, and other changes necessary to implement the paradigmatic model re-

---

7. Schein, *Organizational Culture*, 4.
8. Schein, *Organizational Learning*, 4.
9. Houser, "Executive Board to Strengthen," 22.
10. Cited in Yukl, *Leadership in Organization*, 360.

flected in the broader strategic plan. The focus during convergence is solidifying and reinforcing the strategy established in the reorientation.

Reorientation and convergence processes can be a double-edged sword. Periods of reorientation can result in organization renewal, vitality, and contextual responsiveness. Reorientation can also result in a reckless strategy that breeds intraorganizational division and turf battles. On the other hand, periods of convergence can provide new role clarity, enabling employees and volunteers to carry out the new strategy more effectively. Convergence can enable senior leaders to hire people skilled to implement the needed changes. But periods of convergence can also pose the possibility of reinforcing "the internal forces of stability . . . making it harder for executives to make major changes" in the future.[11] It was, perhaps, the perceived effectiveness and stability of the institutions of the former Mennonite denominations that caused resistance to the changes necessary to realize the missional future of the new denomination.

USING FRAMES

In their 1996 article *Ambidextrous Organizations*, Michael Tushman and Charles O'Reilly developed a theory that organizations need not only evolutionary change but also *revolutionary* or "frame-breaking" change. Reorientation and convergence remain sequential, but leaders need to pay attention to both at the same time, anticipating periods of reorientation well in advance of a downturn in performance. Successful leadership brings increasing alignment among strategy, structure, culture, and process while at the same time preparing for the inevitable revolutions required by discontinuous changes outside the organization.

One wonders if the two former denominations that merged to create Mennonite Church USA adequately assessed the paradigms under which each had been functioning and what kinds of frame-breaking changes the new paradigm would require. It is possible that the lack of systemic health in two key areas contributed to an arrested change process for Mennonite Church USA, which resulted in a six-year period of growing uncertainty and instability: (1) the lack of capacity to perceive and test reality and (2) the lack of capacity to adapt and maintain itself in the face of internal and external changes.

11. Ibid.

In their 1997 book *Reframing Organizations*, Lee Bolman and Terrence Deal offer a paradigm of four frames through which leaders and members can view their organizations: structural, human resources, political, and symbolic. Most organizations will normally identify with one or two of these frames, so looking at the organization through a frame that is less familiar can help leaders determine how resistance to change might become an asset to the change process rather than an obstacle, what new strategic avenues might be explored, and how the leaders' own self-understanding might be broadened.

For example, if leaders prefer to view the organization through the structural or political frame, in times of reorientation they might shift to viewing the organization through the symbolic frame and begin to talk about the future in terms of a story that captures the imagination of the organization. Such an attempt was made in Conrad Kanagy's 2007 profile of Mennonite Church USA, *Road Signs for the Journey*, in which the demographic picture of Mennonite Church USA was described with parallel, metaphoric pictures that recalled the story of Israel's developing history from homeland to fall and exile.

This opens the possibility that organizational effectiveness, growth, and success do not need to be limited by the traits, giftedness, and skill set of the leader. Though leaders have preferred ways of being and may not be able to become all things to all people, Bolman and Deal offer ways for leaders to view their organizations that are not bounded by traits, skill sets, or giftedness alone. Their theory places the organization in a subjective rather than an objective position: with the organization viewed as a subject, leaders can stand outside it, view it from multiple vantage points, and consider how it looks from the perspective of each frame. Leadership itself can be considered subjectively. The leadership team or oversight board can view the organization from multiple and less familiar frames to consider how the preferred leadership frame is limiting or releasing the organization's fuller potential. Competency in viewing organizations through alternating or multiple frames contributes to building greater systemic health.

Getting closer to the ecclesial field and building on organizational research, Jim Herrington, Mike Bonem, and James Furr, synthesized organizational change theory and missional ecclesiology to develop a guide for leading change in churches, outlined in their 2000 book, *Leading Congregational Change*. This approach to leading change is an attempt to align with a missional ecclesiology by framing the issue of change in a set of key questions: What is God doing in this context? What unique gifts and opportunities does this congregation have? How can leaders develop the greatest possible alignment between opportunity, structure, people, and processes?

Though this process is decidedly leader-centered, a key element in leading change is the creation of a vision community. A vision community "is a diverse group of key members who become a committed and trusted community in order to discern and implement God's vision for the congregation."[12] The vision community is an informal structure. The members are not elected nor do they have terms. In fact, they function from the beginning of the process to the end.

In one of the former Mennonite denominations, such a vision community, called the Faith, Life and Strategy Committee, was a long-standing prophetic voice in the denomination. In contrast, the design team for the creation of Mennonite Church USA was made up of leaders who held high-level executive offices in the former denominations and therefore had stakes in the new organization. Interestingly, it was not apparent in the organizational structure of Mennonite Church USA at the time of this study where the work of vision is lodged.

It is possible that in light of the recent declaration of the denomination's Executive Board, an ad hoc vision community of people outside the formal structure could have helped the system become more supportive of the missional future that the denomination is seeking to embody.

ORGANIZATIONS AS LEARNING COMMUNITIES

Theorists such as Margaret Wheatley and Mary Jo Hatch have offered new approaches to organizational learning that are more in touch with postmodern understandings. In this approach, social systems are allowed to organize themselves as living systems rather than as machines. Life organizes itself as it recognizes shared interests and changes in meaning, when the freedom to choose is honored, and when the system is connected more to itself. In a similar vein to the discussion of dialogue, Wheatley advocates for the need and power of deep conversation in developing understanding in organizations. This is clearly informed

---

12. Herrington, Bonem, and Furr, *Leading Congregational Change*, 41.

by the educational theories of progressivism, multiculturalism, and constructivism, which tend to be highly context-sensitive.

Our notion of understanding integrates knowing, acting, and being. Understanding of practice, then, is enacted in and through practice. Such embodied understanding of professional practice constitutes an unfolding "professional way-of-being." In other words, an organizational leader not only learns knowledge and skills, but these are renewed over time as they are integrated into the leader's practice.

Because organizations do not generally function in the classroom, most organizational learning occurs in practice. It is therefore largely self-directed. In *The Courage to Teach*, Parker Palmer calls for learning to happen in a subject-centered community of truth that focuses less on pristine objects of knowledge and ultimate authorities: "In the community of truth . . . truth does not reside primarily in propositions and education is more than delivering propositions about objects to passive auditors."[13] This understanding of self-directed learning in organizations fits well with the work of Bolman and Deal, who recommend that organizational leaders learn not to view their organizations objectively, as though there is a perfect structure or culture to be created. Rather, the goal is to build the capacity to view the organization subjectively by seeing it through multiple frames.

Palmer argues for a counter-cultural approach to learning: "In the community of truth, knowing and teaching and learning look less like General Motors and more like a town meeting, less like bureaucracy and more like bedlam." The method at the center of his community of truth is anti-hierarchical where complex communication results in "sharing observations and interpretations, correcting and complementing each other, torn by conflict in this moment and joined by consensus the next."[14]

Organizations *may* get by without becoming learning communities if all that is needed is adaptive change. In the attempt to adopt a missional ecclesiology, Mennonite Church USA is pursuing transformative change. As seen earlier, Schein identifies the four factors that indicate systemic health: "(1) a sense of identity, purpose, or mission; (2) a capacity on the part of the system to adapt and maintain itself in the face of internal and external changes; (3) a capacity to perceive and test reality;

---

13. Palmer, *Courage to Teach*, 101.
14. Ibid.

and (4) some degree of internal integration or alignment of the subsystems that make up the total system." These four factors are "the basics of a 'capacity to learn.'"[15] The degree to which these factors are developed in an organization will in large part determine its ability to learn and change.

The attempt to create a new denomination based on a missional ecclesiology was intended to result in transformative change based on generative learning. The key learning model embedded in the formational documents of Mennonite Church USA intended to affect transformative change in the learning community. Unfortunately this did not happen.

As the ground begins to shift under denominations, and if the complexity of current social contexts is characterized by discontinuous change, and if Schein is right that one of the "main consequences of technological complexity, globalism, and universal transparency is that some of the old assumptions no longer work,"[16] then organizations of all sizes need to develop the capacity for generative learning that moves the organization beyond maintenance and creates the open space that can result in organizational transformation.

---

15. Schein, *Organizational Learning*, 4
16. Schein, *Three Cultures*.

2

Missional Ecclesiology

THE HEART OF THE issue in this book is the nature of the missional churches of many cultures that the denomination seeks to develop. Ecclesiology deals with the basic assumptions about the nature of the church in its historical context. The emphases in any ecclesiology have given rise to every identifiable tradition, denomination, division, and sect in Christian history. With a history of almost two thousand years, the nature of the church has been framed in countless ways.

Ecclesiology has been described from various disciplinary perspectives. For example, broad ecclesiologies are written from the perspective of missiology and theology, history, and organizational development. Others frame ecclesiology in terms of church tradition, that is, church as sacrament and sign. "Free Church" thinkers cast ecclesiology in terms of voluntary communion. Still others frame ecclesiology in metaphoric trinitarian terms in which the nature of the Father, Son, and Holy Spirit relationship is paralleled in the nature of the church. As is evident, it is impossible to talk about one ecclesiology, for the church has many.

Theologian Neil Ormerod has aptly said, "Of all the theologies, ecclesiology must be the most practical."[1] The nature of the church, as a historical organization, cannot be understood apart from its historical context. While we need to understand the theological foundations of a missional ecclesiology, common understanding about the nature of churches being planted in the contemporary North American context is our focus here.

---

1. Ormerd, "Structure of a Systematic Ecclessiology," 10.

EFFECTS OF POST-CHRISTENDOM ON ECCLESIOLOGY

Post-Christendom first appears in the literature in a 1965 *Interpretation* article by Paul Peachey, "New Ethical Possibility." In this article, he rejects the commonly used "post-Christian" label to describe Western society. He suggests that "post-Christian" indicates the "passing of the 'Christian religion' as such, which would be an obvious fallacy," since the Christian faith *precedes* the rise of Christendom.

Christendom describes a 1,500-year period beginning with Constantine's Edict of Milan, AD 313. By the end of the fourth century, under the reign of Theodosius, the church and society became co-extensive, that is, the church ceased to be different from the society in which it existed. In his correction of David Bosch's benchmark work on the mission of the church, Alan Kreider developed his argument for dividing church history into three epochs: pre-Christendom, Christendom, and post-Christendom. In *Beyond Bosch*, he characterizes the pre-Christendom church as a largely illegal religious group that existed on the margins of society. The church grew through attraction. Membership was voluntary and often involved risk.

Constantine's Edict of Milan, legalizing Christianity, and the determination of Theodosius I in 380 that Christianity would become the official religion of the empire, transformed the nature of the church "from being perceived as a threat to the security of the empire into a guardian of the status quo."[2] This shift in the church's self-understanding defined its ecclesiology for the next 1,500 years. Notable movements such as the Donatists, Waldensians, Lollards, and the Anabaptists were exceptional traditions within normative Christendom. These movements existed as marginal, deviant movements reflective of the pre-Christendom church.

During Christendom, the state and the church became united in making Christianity compulsory for the citizenry of the nation. Beginning with the Protestant Reformation of the sixteenth century, the survival of Christendom received its first serious challenge. While contesting some of the medieval church's practices, the Protestant Reformation retained the hope that church and state would be co-extensive. When the lines of the church are demarked by the lines of the nation, the nature of the

---

2. Shenk, "New Wineskins," 74.

church and mission is formed accordingly. In fact, the church loses any definable sense of mission as central to its being.

In her review of Peri Rasolondraibe's 2001 presentation of "Lutheran Position on Ecclesiology and Mission," Tiina Ahonen summarizes three paradigms in Lutheran history that reflect the move from Christendom to post-Christendom.[3] The first she labels "church without a mission." In this paradigm the church believed that mission was largely a "function of the state." The church did not think about sending missionaries to evangelize the world beyond the boundaries of the state. Instead, whenever the state expanded its boundaries, the church moved into that area and announced her claim on the region as under the reign of Christ.

The second paradigm, "mission without a church," reflects the revival movements that took place in the eighteenth and nineteenth centuries apart from the institutionalized mainline churches. These movements have been referred to as "sodalities," a term popularized by Ralph Winter referring to "mission societies that were created by like-minded entrepreneurs focusing on one or two mission issues."[4]

The third paradigm, "the church in mission," refers to the current era beginning in the second half of the twentieth century in which the disciplines of ecclesiology and missiology began to take each other seriously. This last paradigm is illustrative of Emil Brunner's oft-quoted statement "The church exists by mission, just as fire exists by burning."[5] More than forty years ago Mennonite theologian John Howard Yoder warned regarding what becomes of the church when it loses track of the centrality of mission to its sense of being: "A human community which is not constantly both experiencing and proclaiming the transformation of the human situation by the coming of God among [humans] will immediately degenerate into Judaism or paganism; into defensive moralism or the superstitious practice of 'religion.'"[6]

Reflecting on the shift between the "mission without a church" paradigm to the "church in mission" paradigm, Theologian Lois Barrett offers this interesting eflection on sodalities and Anabaptist ecclesiology:

---

3. Ahonen, "Antedating Missional Church," 574.
4. Pierson, "Beyond Sodalities and Modalities," 299.
5. Brunner, *The Word and the World*, 108.
6. Yoder, "Theology of the Church's Mission," 31.

The Anabaptist movement did not begin as a sodality, to use the term anachronistically. It saw itself as the church, not as an arm of the church. In fact, most Anabaptist leaders emphatically rejected the idea that the magisterial reformers and the Roman Catholics were the church at all. The witness of the Anabaptist movement was completely integral to the Anabaptist congregation (*Gemeinde*; they did not use the German word for church, *Kirche*, to refer to themselves). They had no mission agency, and they were not the mission agency of other reformers.[7]

It is interesting to think about how the organizational culture, structures, and strategy of Mennonite Church USA might have been shaped if more clarity had been given to this historical perspective on a historic Anabaptist ecclesiology in operation during Christendom as a post-Christendom age emerges.

The foundations of Christendom began to crumble in the late nineteenth century, with a convergence of many factors contributing to this collapse. A series of historic movements set the stage for the end of Christendom. Beginning with the Renaissance, next to the Reformation, and down through the Enlightenment, the Industrial Revolution and the possibility of national autonomy all posed mounting challenges to Christendom's self-preserving powers.

Today, a number of trends and anti-trends observable in Western societies have been juxtaposed as a way of describing the emerging post-Christendom context. These trends and anti-trends create paradoxical points of tension within which to understand the end of Christendom. These trends and anti-trends include globalization and nationalism, secularization and new religiosity, privatized religion and an increasingly religious secular life, individualism and new community movements, religious relativism and the desire for simplicity, and clearness and truth.[8] The possibilities of these divergent realities existing together at the same time in the same society are a reflection that it is no longer possible to talk about an expectation that the world is moving toward Christian normalization.

---

7. Barrett, e-mail correspondence with the author. June 4, 2008.
8. Hempelmann, "Context of Christian Witness," 45–46.

The trends and anti-trends of secularization and new religiosity; privatized religion and increasingly secularized life; and individualism and new community movements have had a dramatic effect on traditional meanings of church membership. Building on the work of Paul Hiebert and Darrel Guder, church-planting expert Stuart Murray proposes the need for a "centered-set" model of ecclesiology that speaks to the issues of belonging, believing, and behaving. In contrast to what he calls the "fuzzy-set" church characterized by twentieth-century liberalism, Murray describes a centered-set church as one that embraces a "non-negotiable set of core convictions, rooted in the story which has shaped the community, ultimately in Jesus Christ." This center provides a "focal point, around which members of the community gather enthusiastically." These core convictions define the church as something different from the context surrounding it. Because the congregation has this clear self-definition, the church is freed from fixating on boundaries of exclusion and can "be inclusive, hospitable to others, who are welcome to explore the community."[9]

This description of the centered-set church provides a useful path for churches struggling to understand the nature of belonging to the Christian community at the nexus of the trends and anti-trends in a society that increasingly reflects post-Christendom. Though acknowledging that Christendom for most Americans is past, theologian Patrick Keifert writes, "While Christianity in North America has undergone several disestablishments in the last 200 years, it is hard to see the present culture devoid of Christian influence in its woof and warp."[10] Christianity remains a strong influence in social and political organizations. Few, however, would disagree that the church is moving to the margins of an increasingly multicultural, pluralistic society marked by spiritual ambiguity. Rather than lament this marginalization as though the church is losing ground, many today are embracing post-Christendom as a new opportunity for the church to recover its pre-Christendom identity of solidarity with the marginalized and an opportunity for new levels of creative initiative in mission.

In his 2004 article "Mission from the Margins" in *International Review of Mission*, Philip Wickeri indicates that whether or not we are in a post-Christendom society, the church is being moved to the mar-

9. Murray, *Church After Christendom*, 26–38.
10. Keifert, *We Are Here Now*, 25.

gins. For the church to meet the challenges of its current social context, churches need "a kenosis (or self-emptying) of mission so that they can once again become part of a movement in society that shakes up institutions and calls them to renewal. Our structures need to be more pluriform and de-centralized. In the future, the church may have a lower visibility than it now has; it may, at times, become more "hidden" in social movements. This is part of the *missio Dei*."

THE MISSIONAL SHIFT

Missional theology is a relatively new development in churchly conversations, though it has been a developing paradigm for missiology *and* ecclesiology since the first third of the twentieth century. It is perhaps not new at all, but a revival of a pre-Christendom ecclesiology described by Historian Alan Kreider and/or the recovery of an ecclesiology that reemerged in movements such as the Donatists, Waldensians, Lollards, and Anabaptists. Much of church planting in the second half of the twentieth century was built on "Christendom" assumptions. That is, if you plant a new church at a strategic location, people would come. Contextual sensitivities were a secondary concern. A missional ecclesiology shifts the starting place for the development of new congregations from replicating existing congregations in new locations to investigating how the church will be uniquely incarnated in a new context, given the unique character of that context.

Central to missional theology is a commitment to contextualization in anticipation of Christendom's demise. Missiologist Andrew Walls speaks of two principles that are simultaneously at work when the gospel is being presented to any context. The first is the "indigenizing" principle, which suggests that "the Gospel is at home in every culture and every culture is at home with the Gospel." The second is the "pilgrim" principle, which suggests that "the Gospel will also put us out of step with society."[11] These principles are a sharp contrast to the Christendom model of mission as social and cultural conquest.

The task of contextualization in post-Christendom poses a challenge to ways of doing mission for traditional denominations. Professor of Congregational Mission Craig Van Gelder chronicles the shifting roles that denominations have played since the Protestant Reformation.

---

11. Walls, *Missionary Movement*, 7–8.

The function and benefits of the church have been called into question in recent decades, marked by the decline of denominations.[12] In his 2001 dissertation, *Identity or Mission*, Layne Lebo provides an example within the context of the Brethren in Christ Church—a denomination closely related to Mennonite Church USA. The Brethren in Christ denomination finds itself wrestling with the tension of retaining the foundational values on which the denomination was based while at the same time responding to a context that is asking for new forms. Lebo raises the question, Which factor will be the dominant influence in historic denominations and shape the church's work: identity or mission?

Missional theology would suggest that this question poses a false dichotomy; the identity of the church *is* mission. Nevertheless, the question describes well the crucible in which denominations function in a post-Christendom context. Many churches in the West have become institutionalized to the point that the preservation of the tradition, or institutional identity, competes in influence with the needs and opportunities presented by the mission context. Managing the tension of the indigenizing and pilgrim principles can offer an important corrective to the nature of churches and denominations that reflect a post-Christendom penchant for institutionalization.

The roots of missional theology are found in the work of Karl Barth's presentations at the Brandenburg Missionary Conference in 1932. At this conference Barth shifted the Enlightenment-era conversation from talking about mission as an activity of the church to mission as an activity of God. In his benchmark book, *Transforming Mission*, David Bosch wrote that this way of speaking about mission resulted in a new theological paradigm, "which broke radically with an Enlightenment approach to theology."[13] Barth's understanding of mission as an activity of God was further developed by Karl Hartenstein. And several decades later, at the International Missionary Conference at Willingen, Germany, in 1952, building on the foundational work of Barth and Hartenstein, the idea of *missio Dei* was described: "The ... doctrine of *missio Dei* was articulated at this conference: The classical doctrine of the *missio Dei* as God the

---

12. Van Gelder, "Rethinking Denominations," 30.
13. Bosch, *Transforming Mission*, 390.

Father sending the Son, and God the Father and the Son sending the Spirit was expanded to include yet another 'movement': Father, Son, and Holy Spirit sending the church into the world."[14]

Now mission was understood as *participation* in the sending of God rather than originating in the imagination of the church. The church's mission has no life of its own: "The genetic code of the missional church makes it missionary in its very essence," Van Gelder says.[15] In this new concept, mission is not primarily an act of the church but "an attribute of God."[16] The nature of the church is no longer understood in imperial terms as a power seeking to normalize Christianity.

Borrowing from theologian Lesslie Newbigin to extend this paradigm, Missiologist Art McPhee writes that God's people are involved in mission not out of obligation but out of a new identity: "When Jesus said, 'You will be my witnesses' (Acts 1:8), he was not issuing a command but making a statement about the nature of his followers. Likewise the New Testament's metaphors for believers—salt, light, fishers, stars, letters, ambassadors, good seed—are never made in the imperatives. They are always *indicative*, attesting that mission is the natural activity of the church."[17]

Perhaps no one has done more to articulate an accessible understanding of missional theology than missiologist Wilbert Shenk. He articulated it most succinctly within an Anabaptist framework in his 2000 pamphlet, *Ten Defining Themes in Anabaptist Mission Theology*. In Shenk's defining themes, we see the development of a missional theology that is built on the foundational work of Newbigin's trinitarian missiology. Beginning with an understanding of mission originating in God's mission, Shenk ties the mission of God to a messianic movement characterized by the suffering servant paradigm most fully revealed in Jesus, the gospel of peace. The church as sent by Jesus, suffering servant and messiah, is the primary "carrier and instrument" of the messianic purpose." As primary carrier and instrument, Shenk says that the mission of God will move the church into "deep penetration into the world – for the world, against the world." This understanding of mission is charac-

---

14. Ibid.
15. Van Gelder, *Missional Church*, 33.
16. Bosch, *Transforming Mission*, 390.
17. McPhee, "*Missio Dei*," 10 (emphasis added).

terized by "radical obedience and discipleship."[18] Van Gelder reflects on this trinitarian understanding of mission in the missionary age: "The church lives between the times. It lives between the now and the not yet. The redemptive reign of God in Christ is already present, meaning that the power of God is fully manifested in the world through the gospel under the leading of the Holy Spirit."[19]

Lois Barrett writes of the growing influence of missional ecclesiology in many denominations, particularly mainline Protestant denominations. Mainline Protestant—and for that matter, evangelical—groups are for the first time trying to understand what it means to be the church in a society where the church's power is marginalized. Barrett celebrates this reality as a sure sign of the end of Constantinian Christendom. This, she says, liberates the church to pay closer attention to the church's context and the needs of the world: "Freed of the need to make things come out 'right' for the government or society or to feel at home in the culture, the missional church can live out its understanding of the gospel of Jesus Christ. The church can have a different worldview. It can become an alternative community. It is different from the world, not for the sake of being different, but because it is seeking to conform to the life, death, and resurrection of Jesus Christ, rather than to conform to the surrounding culture."[20]

Echoing the developing missional paradigm grounded in the Trinity, Barrett concludes, "The witness of the missional church is always grounded in the gospel of Christ, initiated by God, and led by the Holy Spirit."[21]

Working in the context of acute post-Christendom England, Murray understands *missio Dei* and its resultant missional church in similar terms. Mission flows from the character and purposes of God. The broad work of *missio Dei* should not be reduced to evangelism or church planting. Rather *missio Dei* calls forth a church characterized by the incarnation of Jesus. Churches that are planted need not only to proclaim the good news, but also to be good news or be a sign of the good news to the contexts in which they live. All missionary churches should be distinctive and engaged.

18. Shenk, *Ten Defining Themes*, 9.
19. Van Gelder, *Missional Church*, 33.
20. Barrett, "Authentic Witness," 181.
21. Ibid., 182.

Because of the frame-breaking, highly contextual, and incarnational nature of a missional ecclesiology, it is often not easy to predict how this ecclesiology will be fleshed out in terms of practices to be replicated in multiple contexts. Barrett believes that the best way to identify practices is through observation intent on distilling patterns—or indicators—of missional ecclesiology demonstrated by churches seeking to live out *missio Dei*. Her research demonstrates how case studies of missional churches provide what Bent Flyvbjerg refers to as the "force of example" in understanding the nature of a phenomenon.[22] In her empirical research, Barrett has identified twelve indicators of a missional church (see appendix B).

The missional church understands reconciliation to be work that originates with God. The church bears witness to this work that God is doing in the world. Where the church is involved in the work of reconciliation, it does so as sign and witness. As Alan and Eleanor Kreider and Paulus Widjaja write, "After all, our mission as Christians is not primarily to bring solutions to the world's problems, but to bring hope for redemption."[23] The church takes up residence at the places yet to be reconciled to God to proclaim and be a sign of the reign that God is bringing to bear on all creation. The hope of the missional church's witness is that, upon seeing and hearing, those not reconciled to God will seek the reconciliation that God offers through Jesus. A missional ecclesiology cuts a path between tendencies to cast the church as builder of the kingdom, on the one hand, and tendencies that cast the church as the lifeboat for a world that is a sinking ship, on the other.

MISSIONAL ECCLESIOLOGY AND MENNONITE CHURCH USA

A missional ecclesiology is the declared foundational theological frame for Mennonite Church USA: "Joining in God's activity in the world, [we] develop and nurture missional Mennonite congregations of many cultures." There are several ways in which missional theology is well suited to Mennonite Church ecclesiology. First, Mennonites have historically approached the Bible from a Christocentric perspective, that is, Scripture is read and interpreted through the lens of the gospel. Church planting grounded in *missio Dei* does not look to Acts and the Epistles

---

22. Flyvbjerg, "Five Misunderstandings," 228.
23. Kreider, Kreider, and Widjaja, *Culture of Peace*, 79.

to provide the roadmap for church-planting principles, as seen in many replication-based church planting strategies. The church instead seeks to incarnate a contextually relevant mission that originates in the character of God as revealed in Jesus.

Second, Mennonites have a five-hundred-year history of life and witness from the margins. They maintain a deeply held conviction that the church is to be separate from the state. If Barrett is right, then the church liberated from "the need to make things come out right for the government or society or to feel at home in culture" should provide a natural orientation for how Mennonites seek to plant new congregations.[24]

Third, Mennonites have historically maintained an identity as a martyr church and therefore have emphasized what Shenk proposes as a radical obedience and discipleship that penetrates deeply into the world. They maintain a strong identity as resident aliens in a two-kingdom universe. Operating from the margins has been the modus operandi for the Mennonite tradition throughout its history.

A number of publications have been produced for churches within Mennonite Church USA in an attempt to form the new denomination toward a missional ecclesiology. However, at the point of the six-year review, the Executive Board of the denomination acknowledged that the church had not yet realized a missional identity, "declaring that our vision and call to engage in God's purposes in the world is not adequately supported by our present relationships, behaviors and organization."[25]

To become a missional church, "the organizational self-understanding of the denominational, organizational church is replaced by a missional self-understanding for the missional church," Van Gelder writes.[26] It is not easy to effect ecclesiological change in a denominational organization whose basic assumptions have evolved over 450 years, influenced by the melting pot of ecclesiologies present in the North American context.

---

24. Barrett, "Authentic Witness," 181.
25. Houser, "Executive Board to Strengthen," 22.
26. Van Gelder, "Rethinking Denominations," 31.

3

Church Planting

HAVING CONSIDERED THE IMPLICATIONS of a missional ecclesiology and the contributions of organizational development theory, we now turn to issues related to church planting. Church planting has been defined by Conrad Kanagy as "initiatives to develop new congregations, fellowships, or house church/simple churches."[1] This term is contested by some as less specific than labels such as "new church starts" or "emerging communities of faith." While there is a great deal of literature written on the subject of church planting, much of what is written is not scholarly research. In many cases, church-planting literature is generated by a practitioner who has experienced a measure of "success" and written a book to describe his or her approach to new church development. This is sometimes done in preparation for, or as a result of, requests to offer instruction to other potential church planters and/or denominational or parachurch mission entities. Perhaps the lack of scholarly literature and journals in the field is due in part to the possibility that those drawn to the field of church planting tend to be entrepreneurial in spirit, that is, they are perhaps more comfortable in the realms of doing and building rather than reflecting and theorizing.

In recent years, a few practitioner-researchers have begun to conduct empirical research in the area of church planting. For example, Ed Stetzer and Philip Connor's research has identified four significant factors associated with church-plant survivability among church plants in the Southern Baptist Convention. These factors examine how closely "the church plant expectations meet the reality of the church planting experience, the extent to which church planters provide leadership development for new church members, the consistency with which a

---

1. Kanagy, *Profile of Mennonite*, 3.

church planter meets with a group of church planting peers, and the development of a proactive stewardship development plan."[2]

Much more research is needed to understand the experience of church planting in North America, especially regarding "the complexities and contradictions of real life."[3]

CONTEXTUAL ISSUES

Contextual understanding is an important issue in the development of new churches. Much of church planting occurs in minority and immigrant cultures as established Christian churches attempt to bring a distinctive theological understanding of the gospel to these groups. Contextualizing these theological understandings is a complicated task. For example, Twyla Hernandez found that the three most important missiological needs for a Latin American subculture in the United States are church planting, leadership development, and increased social ministries.

Attention to whether the targeted context for the development of a new church is urban or rural is also important. In his 2000 study, *Planting Churches in Small Towns and Rural Areas*, Thomas Nebel suggested that because of "rural rebound," rural and small-town communities ought to be considered strategic places for new churches that will meet the needs of the newly burgeoning populations in these areas. He argues that the church planter's strategies for developing new congregations must be contextualized to the unique sociology of rural communities and small towns.

This concern for interpreting the context in which churches are being planted dovetails with the contextual nature of missional ecclesiology. Approaches to church planting informed by Christendom will assume the church itself is a cultural paradigm and will impose the culture of the church on the context in which the church is being planted. On the contrary, the post-Christendom church understands itself to have an "essence" awaiting contextual incarnation.

---

2. Stetzer and Connor, *Church Plant Survivability*, 14.
3. Flyvbjerg, "Five Misunderstandings," 237.

STRATEGY

The greatest attention in the area of church planting has been on strategy. Much of this research focuses on answering the questions "Why are church-planting entities *not* more effective in developing new congregations?" and "How can church-planting entities become *more* effective in developing new congregations?" These questions in themselves point to a disappointment with current outcomes.

In his 2004 study, *Facing the Challenge of the Urban Frontier*, Douglas Howells suggests a number of reasons for the lack of effectiveness in the Christian Church's (Disciples of Christ) church-planting work. Revealing a bias that church planting is largely an urban endeavor, he cites the lack of a major presence of established Christian Churches (Disciples of Christ) in urban areas of the United States. In *Creating Multi-congregational Churches*, Jeffrey King proposes a model for increasing church planting effectiveness by developing multicongregations within existing churches in order to multiply a church's ministry with the intended effect of spinning off new churches. And in his dissertation, Martin Kohlbry argues for the development of small groups as a strategy for increasing the effectiveness of church-planting initiatives.

Jervis Payne and Joel Rainey conducted studies to test the effectiveness of several models of church planting. In his comparison study, "An Evaluation of the Systems Approach," Payne identified several areas of concern in need of further theoretical work to foster greater effectiveness in church planting. These areas of concern include clarifying ecclesiology, pneumatology, strategy, and methodology. Rainey examined the effectiveness of church planting by looking at a variety of church-planting models employed, conversion growth rate, the rate of new church starts, and the various contexts in which churches are planted. The most striking finding was that church plants experience an inverted relationship between congregational size and conversion rate. In other words, as a church grows, the rate of conversion growth slows proportionately.

In a qualitative study, "A Strategy for Planting a Church," John Turner examined the possibilities for using the Natural Church Development inventory, an inventory designed for assessing the health of existing congregations, as the foundational, philosophical, and structural paradigm for the development of new congregations. He used narrative inquiry—the analysis of collected stories—to further deepen the understandings developed through the quantitative research of Christian Schwarz reported in Schwarz's *Natural Church Development*.

In an ecclesiological—and therefore theological—pursuit, many students of church planting believe that the foundational paradigm for the effective church planting rests in the Acts of the Apostles and the Epistles of the New Testament that trace the development of the first-century church. These theorists attempt to distill the early church's principles and strategies in order to replicate them as *the* church-planting strategy. While examining the early church helps us understand how the church contextualized the gospel in a pre-Christendom world, this orientation runs the risk of assuming that twenty-first-century contexts are equal to first-century contexts.

In his 2000 book, *Church Planting*, Stuart Murray argues instead that if the church is attempting to proclaim and be a sign of God's reign, the Gospels rather than the Epistles should be the guiding foundational material. In short, the church should attempt to incarnate the mission of God rooted in the gospel of Jesus rather than replicate the models and methodologies of first century churches. Incarnational approaches to church development will seek to develop ministries that holistically reflect the work of Jesus. This understanding of an *incarnational* foundation for church-planting strategy is consistent with the commitments of a missional ecclesiology. The emerging missional church's strategy will be focused on the evangelism, liberation, deliverance, and justice-making ministries in the model of Jesus.

CHURCH PLANTERS

Because church planting is often a leader-centered rather than a democratic initiative, the ecclesiological orientation, gifts, skill sets, and traits of the church planter will determine in large part how the strategy for church planting develops. Work has been done in recent years attempting to identify standard skill sets and personal traits for church planters that are distinguished from the skill set of other types of church leaders. In his 2005 doctoral dissertation, "An Evaluation of Pastoral Self-Leadership and Church Health," Steve Jackson attempted to demonstrate the importance of self-leadership practices or skills in developing healthy congregations. Self-leadership is the ability to reflect on one's own practice to enhance one's performance and leadership competence.

In another doctoral study intended to determine important competencies and personal traits in successful church planters, J. Allen Thompson found that assessors and church planters agreed that leadership, evangelism, preaching, philosophy of ministry, and discipling were the most important skills. Conscientiousness, resiliency, flexibility, likableness, self-image, sensitivity, and dynamism were considered essential character traits for church planters. It should be noted that these skills and traits were identified by a panel of assessment center leaders—those who work in organized programs to assess skill sets of prospective church planters—and a panel of church planters as the most important. Thompson did not determine if, in fact, church planters with these skills and traits are successful in their task.

It is important not only to consider the personal traits and skill sets of church planters but also to consider the unique role of those who develop new congregations. In his doctoral study, Stan Buck looked at the relationship between pastoral tenure and congregational growth in new congregations. The study explored the evolving roles of founding pastors and how these roles need to change over the first twenty years of a church's existence. During this time, the church moves from an emerging to an established paradigm. Buck's finding suggests that church planters should not see themselves only as "starters"; long-term pastorates in emerging congregations resulted in more growth. Another doctoral candidate, David Davis, found that alignment between the self-understanding of the church planter's role and the congregation's expectations for leadership was critical to healthy relationships within developing congregations.

An important issue in the church-planting literature is ongoing leadership development of an effective church planter. Mentoring is believed to be an important part of this. D. Keith Cowart showed that the subjects in his study viewed their mentoring relationships as key components of their preparation. Rafael Hernandez found that theological reflection is a key mentoring practice in helping church planters and their supervisors respond both sensitively and strategically when working in multiethnic contexts. Ronald Turman found that a church planter's ability to involve every member in the life and ministry of the new church contributed to high levels of member commitment. All of this points to a great deal of learning that must take place as a church planter attempts to apply ecclesiology in situ.

Church Planter Competency Development

Few studies have been done that reflect on the issue of how church planters are helped in developing their competency for church planting. Cowart found that sixteen church planters who had planted at least one reproducing church[4] identified mentoring by an experienced church planter to be a key factor in the success of their work. In a case study with one pastor, David Davis found that the assessment of an outside consulting firm enabled the pastor to become more authentic and effective in his leadership. Rafael Hernandez found that "church planting" in a diverse ethno/cultural context required that supervisors and church planters practice theological reflection to develop effective ways of working within the cultural/ethnic urban environment. In another study, Allen Thompson found that both church planters and a panel of assessors were able to identify similar positive characteristics of church planters.

A number of parachurch organizations offer intensive training sessions promising to give church planters a head start on their work. Some of these include Acts 29, Church Multiplication Training Center, "boot camps" sponsored by the Vineyard, and so on. No empirical research can be found that reports the effectiveness of short-term, intensive assessment and training center programs. Of the research available on the way church planters develop understanding about their role and task, it seems that approaches focusing on theological reflection in context, in situ coaching, and mentoring are promising approaches for building competency.

Church Planter and Key Stakeholder Relationships

A pervasive trend in the field of missiology and ecclesiology is the focus on the development of mission partnerships. A society marked increasingly by post-Christendom has resulted in the erosion of the social power bases of mainline Protestant and evangelical churches in American and western European societies. This erosion has had definite implications

---

4. "Reproducing" congregations are often distinguished from "replicating" congregations. Reproducing congregations plant new churches that allow the new congregation to reflect the context in which it is planted. Replicating congregations plant new churches that are intended to replicate the ecclesial model of the parent congregation with little concern for reflecting the sociocultural context in which the new church is being planted.

for many mission efforts that exist as sodalities. It is no longer assumed that mission flows "only across salt water . . . mission is also to the dominant culture."[5] It also follows that mission will no longer flow from the "institutional church" to "the field."

In response to an emerging missional theology and a growing post-denominational movement, ad hoc rather than programmatic partnerships for mission abound. Shant Henry Manuel's study grounded the idea of partnership in the Old Testament in which, true to a paradigm of missional theology, God initiates mission but carries out this mission in covenantal relationships, understood in terms of partnership.

The idea of covenant relationship as a paradigm for mission partnership is significant. In his study of the nature of the mission partnership between the Evangelical Christian Missionary Union and the Christian and Missionary Alliance, Douglas Tiessen found that invitational partnership is based on a joint venture, coming alongside coordination of efforts, cooperation as the goal, and a collaboration of working together. His description of the qualities of invitational partnerships demonstrates a shift from programmatic, agency-based compacts to relational and invitational partnerships.

In spite of this attention given to the importance of partnership in mission, not much information on church planting focuses on the partnership between the church planter and the key stakeholders (that is, regional or denominational mission structures and other supportive partners, as well as members of the fledgling church itself who serve as a point of reference and accountability for the church planter). Literature refers primarily to the teams of people doing the planting and expecting to be part of the new church. In some literature, when the stakeholder groups' role was accountability, it is clear that the author understood these groups to be more obstacle than support. The source of resistance was often found in the way key stakeholders and church planters differed in their perception of what an effective church planter does and in the nature of the church that is being planted.

---

5. Barrett, "Authentic Witness," 181.

COMMON UNDERSTANDING IN DEVELOPING CONGREGATIONS

A key issue in the field of church planting is the way common understanding is developed about the nature of an emerging congregation. Where does common understanding originate when mission originates with God? Who is the bearer of vision in emerging congregations? How is the vision developed in a way that causes the stakeholders to move beyond compliance to commitment? How do the subcultures within a denominational system and within a developing congregation come to common understanding of what they are hoping to do? The answer to these questions might be found in a growing body of literature that speaks to the issues of organizational learning described in chapter 1. Developing common understanding about developing congregations requires competency in two key skills in the learning organization: corporate discernment and dialogue.

Corporate Discernment

Discovering and embracing a missional ecclesiology requires a process that extends beyond the pronouncement of leaders. When the Executive Board of Mennonite Church USA announced the underperformance of the denomination in realizing a missional future, it was signaling a need for greater alignment within the organization. That the organization had been functioning for six years at that point indicated the need for new levels of discernment and the development of more common understanding among the parts of the church.

Developing a common vision for the church is an exercise of corporate discernment at every level. This is no less the case for seeking common understanding among church planters and their key stakeholders with regard to the nature of the church that is being planted. In his doctoral dissertation, Bruce Emmert assessed the effectiveness of a process in which, early in the planning for a church plant, the core group members together discerned the mission, core values, vision, and goals of the new church. His finding were consistent with the organizational culture research base: the process of corporate discernment had a direct impact on ownership, long-term orientation, community, synergy, and sense of accomplishment. The process also moved the group beyond compliance to a high level of commitment characterized by loyalty and high creativity. This confirms the work of organizational specialist Peter Senge: "You're 'committed' when you are not only enrolled but feel fully responsible for making the vision happen."[6] The process described by Emmert also resulted in a feeling of heightened competence on the part of the group's leader.

It is unlikely that the idea of planting a church will be born in the minds of a number of people at the same time. Based on this book's introductory story, it would appear that how this vision emerges and is cultivated, and how it is held by the various stakeholders is a key issue in the vitality and viability of emerging churches. Though visions emerge in unpredictable ways, a misaligned organizational system will be ill-prepared to receive the vision and foster its development.

Dialogue

Organizational specialist Mary Jo Hatch calls into question the assumption that the point of leadership is to manage organizational culture which, in postmodern terms, is interpreted as "control." Because postmodernity is a socially constructed world, "we cannot, as individuals, choose a different reality and impose it on others, the others must participate as well." One social constructivist approach to change and learning is to create an open process that is "available to all via public discourse." If, as postmoderns suggest, "organizations are constructed from language," then dialogue becomes the means by which reality is created.[7] Theologian Harry Huebner writes, "What we say to one another on the way is how the world becomes the world to us."[8] Dialogue enables members of a culture to become "observers of their own thinking."[9]

Because discernment of common understanding among church planters and key stakeholders is a corporate exercise, communication will be the centerpiece of the process. Schein asserts that communication across organizational cultures is necessary for successful organizational development in postmodernity. His assessment of the world from an industrial perspective parallels the global shifts and pluralism of post-

6. Senge, *Fifth Discipline*, 203.
7. Hatch, *Organizational Theory*, 367.
8. Huebner, *Echoes of the Word*, 1.
9. Senge, *Fifth Discipline*, 242.

Christendom in the ecclesial perspective. "We must acknowledge that one of the main consequences of technological complexity, globalism, and universal transparency is that some of the old assumptions no longer work.... We will have to find ways of communicating across cultural boundaries, first by establishing some communication that stimulates mutual understanding rather than mutual blame."[10]

Developing the discipline of dialogue for creating common understanding rather than mutual blame is key to developing common understanding among constituent subcultures. Edgar Schein is emphatic on the essential role that dialogue plays in organizational development: "Dialogue thus becomes a central element of any model of organizational transformation."[11]

What both Schein and Senge are referring to as dialogue is something deeper and more intentional than "discussion." Schein suggests that when an organization finds itself in substantive conversation, the process passes through a point of deliberation where there is disagreement and lack of understanding. The choice to move to discussion begins a process characterized by advocacy, competing, and convincing. This leads to dialectic, where the participants explore oppositions. The process then moves to debate, where the goal is to resolve the opposition by logic, beating the other down, and winning.

On the other hand, for conversation to move to dialogue requires a space for suspending the need for immediate resolution so that participants can listen, accept difference, and build mutual trust. This process then moves to substantive dialogue in which participants confront their own assumptions and the assumptions of the other. The participants are open about their feelings, and they seek to build common ground. At its best, this process leads to what Schein refers to as "metalogue," which is characterized by "thinking and feeling as a whole group, building new assumptions and a new culture."[12]

Senge offers consistent but simplified requirements for healthy dialogue: (1) all participants must "suspend" their assumptions, literally hold them "as if suspended before us"; (2) all participants must regard one another as colleagues; and (3) there must be a "facilitator" who "holds

---

10. Schein, *Three Culture of Management*, par. 51.
11. Schein, "On Dialogue," 27.
12. Ibid., 32.

the context" of dialogue.[13] Taken together with Schein's understanding about the role that basic assumptions play in the development of an organizational culture, the discipline of dialogue is critical to the process of developing common understanding for organizational culture.

If the attempt to create a new organizational culture based on a missional ecclesiology within Mennonite Church USA was arrested due to a lack of alignment, this understanding of dialogue could be an important contributor to new levels of alignment in basic assumption for the executive, interlocutor, and incarnational subcultures. In the same way, in developing a common understanding for a missional ecclesiology for planting churches in complex social contexts, this type of substantive dialogue will be a necessary discipline for church planters and their key stakeholders. Developing common understanding through dialogue is essential to the process of organizational learning and change.

---

13. Senge, *Fifth Discipline*, 226.

Part 2

Perspectives

In 2006, Mennonite Church USA adopted a refined statement of the denomination's purpose: "Joining in God's activity in the world, [we] develop and nurture missional Mennonite congregations of many cultures." While this purpose remains the defining priority of Mennonite Church USA to date, many in the denomination have not experienced this reality.

In an attempt to understand the current state of developing "missional Mennonite congregations of many cultures," I conducted numerous interviews. The first was with denominational leaders and an officer elected by the delegate body. Additional denominational perspective was gained in conversations with a representative of the denominational mission agency. The second interview was conducted with ministry staff members from the regional conference that encompasses the churches in the introductory story and in the four case studies in this book. The participants included the four conference ministry staff members and one elected officer who oversaw developing and credentialing leaders within the conference. These interviews are described, as are the themes that emerged from them, in chapter 4.

Finally, I interviewed church planters and key stakeholders in four churches that have a formal relationship with the regional Midwestern conference of Mennonite Church USA. These church plants represent a diversity of ethnic and rural/urban contexts: among a Hispanic population in a small city, a Hmong population in a major city, an Anglo population in a small city, and a multiethnic group in a major city. The diversity of contexts and ethnicity provide information-rich cases, which are described and discussed in chapters 5 through 8.

4

Denominational and Conference Leaders

ON A DEVELOPING MISSIONAL ECCLESIOLOGY

WHILE MY CONVERSATION WITH conference leaders focused on regional and therefore more concrete experiences than my conversation with denominational leaders, the interviews with both groups surfaced three issues in the development of a missional ecclesiology within Mennonite Church USA: (1) a growing ability to describe a missional ecclesiology (positive missional reflection), (2) examples of anti-missional thinking that threaten to derail the development of a missional ecclesiology, and (3) examples of systemic organizational confusion about how to put a missional ecclesiology into operation throughout the denominational system.

Positive Missional Reflection

Denominational and conference leaders identified five possible ways a missional ecclesiology contributes to a clearer understanding of the mission of Mennonite Church USA: (1) it gives attention to God's preceding work in the world; (2) it creates an understanding of the church as itself sent; (3) it reframes the understanding of hospitality; (4) it encourages contextualization of ministry; and (5) it gives special attention to naming polarities within a given context.

Denominational leaders identified a key attribute of missional ecclesiology in terms of God's mission preceding human activity. As an executive staff member put it, "I regard missional church as a reorientation of our minds and hearts toward asking, 'What is God doing and what is God desiring?' rather than, 'What are we to do and what have we done and how should we do it differently?'" A primary commitment of missional ecclesiology is found in a church that focuses first on God's activity rather than on human activity. Another denominational staff member suggested that this foundational commitment "becomes a renewal movement in which we have a heightened awareness of God's activity that changes our activity, molds our activity, and reaches into every aspect of what we do and say." Missional ecclesiology was seen as orienting the church's worship, education, and systemic relationships in light of God's mission in the world. There was uniform agreement among conference leaders that a missional ecclesiology would be shaped by an understanding that God's preceding mission sets the agenda for the church's mission.

A conference staff member said, "To be missional means that we are joining God's reconciling work in the world. God is at work to reconcile people to himself, to each other, and to creation. The missional church joins in that work." A conference minister offered his confirmation by saying that to be missional means "embracing God's big dream for the world. God is renewing all things to himself in Christ and the church; being missional is embracing that. By embracing that, I meant participation [in that]."

Another key attribute of missional ecclesiology as described by denominational and conference leaders is the understanding of the church as no longer sending people out into mission; the church itself is sent. A denominational leader put it this way: "It means that we can no longer take a perspective that we pay someone to do our . . . outreach work for us. We are compelled to look at what God is already doing in our community. . . . It's not something far away; it is something in our community." This leader described the "sent" nature of the missional church as "turning our chairs around to those outside the circle." This turning around results in an openness to change, taking risks, trying, and failing. Missional ecclesiology is reflected in "a church that is confident that God's presence is with us . . . even if we don't quite know what God is up to."

One denominational leader identified that embracing a missional ecclesiology requires a fundamental shift in orientation, saying, "The very common thought about a congregation is that it is *our* congregation, it's there for us, we determine what happens there." The elected officer of the denomination called for a paradigm shift in a long-cherished value within the Mennonite church of the "priesthood of all believers." For a long time, many in the Mennonite church have wrongly interpreted the priesthood of all believers to mean that the church should have a flat hierarchy of leadership. A missional perspective of the priesthood of all believers has less to do with church governance and everything to do with mission. The officer went on to assert, "A missional understanding of the priesthood of all believers means that 'we are all now commissioned' to participate in God's mission." She suggested that this is very different from a former "generation, where you send the missionaries, *you* commission *them*."

The newness of this idea and its growing influence among conference leaders was revealed in a comment by the executive conference minister: "I've recently been talking about the church not as the 'church with a mission,' but the church as 'missionary' being about God's ministry in the world [as] an end. . . . The church is not an end. The church is the means." These reflections suggest that there is growing awareness of what is being said in the scholarly literature and that it is becoming a part of the denomination's and conference's conceptual paradigm.

In a missional frame, a particular understanding of hospitality becomes a core value that determines the shape of mission. A denominational staff member suggested that a key benchmark for Mennonite Church USA's embodiment of a missional ecclesiology "is seen in its ability to accept the world's hospitality, being a guest of the world. The encounter of the world happens at their bidding and not our definition." The foundational questions asked by those leading from a missional perspective included "Where would [the community in which I live] most welcome me? What hospitality do I need to accept?" The paradigm offered here for hospitality was the sending out of the seventy:

> Carry no purse, no bag, no sandals; and greet no one on the road. Whatever house you enter, first say, "Peace to this house!" And if anyone is there who shares in peace, your peace will rest on that person; but if not, it will return to you. Remain in the same house, eating and drinking whatever they provide, for the laborer deserves to be paid. Do not move about from house to house. Whenever you enter a town and its people welcome you, eat what is set before you. (Luke 10:4–8)

Understanding how to accept the world's hospitality is a highly contextual matter. Denominational leaders suggested that an inherent aspect of a missional ecclesiology is a focus on contextualization of ministry. This is both the promise and the peril of embracing a missional ecclesiology. One denominational staff member said, "I understand the missional thrust to be recontextualized everywhere." This can make it difficult to speak of ministry with any kind of generalization. One denominational leader attempted to characterize the kinds of questions people ask when viewing ministry from a missional frame: "What are peoples' passions in the community where I am? Even things like 'Does everybody show up for the football game'? What are the life needs of the people? Are they poor? Are they complacently rich? What is their educational level?"

A further refinement of the issue of contextualization of ministry is the specific attention the missional church pays to the polarities within a given context in order to bring healing and hope as a witness to the nearness of God's reign. The vision statement of Mennonite Church USA is "God calls us to be followers of Jesus Christ and, by the power of the Holy Spirit, to grow as communities of grace, joy, and peace, so that God's healing and hope flow through us to the world."[1] The operational commitments of this vision will result in churches that look for polarizations present in the community that are in need of reconciliation and bring healing and hope as a witness to the nearness of God's reign. Denominational and conference leaders offer examples of these polarizations including immigration, racism, and the gap between rich and poor.

Identified polarities extend not only to gaps "in the world" but also to gaps within the ecumenical church, what one might refer to as "ecclesiastical tribalism," or the increasing redistribution of Christians into like-minded congregations in light of decreasing denominational loyalty. The elected officer of Mennonite Church USA suggested that bringing healing and hope to these polarities is "bringing the good news of salvation through Jesus Christ. If we don't bring healing and hope, we don't bring good news."

Anti-Missional Reflection

As denominational and conference leaders shared their thoughts on missional ecclesiology, they identified a number of issues that threaten

---

1. Mennonite Church USA Executive Board, *Mennonite Church USA 2020*, par. 1.

to derail the development of a missional ecclesiology within Mennonite Church USA. Issues identified by denominational leaders included (1) constituents who see the church primarily as a vendor of therapeutic services, (2) the allure of acculturation to American individualism, and (3) a historically formed inability to receive the world's hospitality. Among conference leaders, two issues persist that are inconsistent with a missional ecclesiology: (1) an expectation for "successful" church planting and (2) a penchant for replicating forms of ministry.

Among Mennonites in the current generation, denominational leaders identified a growing expectation to see the church as a vendor of therapeutic services. The question has shifted from "How does the church help me to live out the call of Jesus?" to "How does the church help me to live the life I've chosen a little bit better?" The elected officer described this phenomenon: "We have bought into American psychology. 'What's in it for me? I don't want to be bothered; I don't want to be moved, shaken, stretched. I like it just for me.' This is in direct opposition to the missional church." An executive leader made a similar observation: "The church becomes a safe haven to soothe us so we can return to the complexity of family and work and society." Mennonites seem to be looking to the church for the "benefit of supporting *my* faith and need for relationships with others who have a faith around certain definitions and customs. That may not be the ideal, but I think it's the real."

Another issue that threatens to derail the development of a missional ecclesiology within Mennonite Church USA is the increasing acculturation of separatist Mennonites to American individualism. One denominational staff member suggested that Mennonites are moving away from a historic identity as alien and stranger to the world: "We're way too comfortable. And every bit as strong as the impulse was in the past to be separate from, is now an impulse to blend in; we don't want to be different." Starkly stated, church members see the church's mission "at the worst end of the scale, as being functional until I am gone."

While an understanding of hospitality is a core element of missional ecclesiology, the denominational leaders questioned whether Mennonites in the current generation are able to embrace the paradigm shift from *extending* hospitality to *receiving* hospitality. Citing research conducted by a consultant hired to guide the framing of the new denomination, an executive leader characterized the experience of Mennonites and hospitality: "Mennonites are wonderful if you identify hospitality in 'coming to be with us.' But we are terrible in . . . accepting others' hospitality. In other words, Mennonites understand hospitality as accepting other people into Mennonite space as long as the space remains *our* space."

Conference leaders said that an expectation of "success" in church planting persists within the conference. "Success" was understood in specific terms assuming that when a church is planted, it will prosper and grow in a linear fashion, requiring little attention to its reason for being. An elected conference officer wondered,

> What paradigm is behind the thinking on [church planting]? If we plant a church, is it destined to grow and survive and flourish? If you look at history, lots of churches mentioned in the New Testament seemed to have disappeared within one hundred years or something. I compare this to an article I read not too long ago about planning a restaurant. . . . Something like two-thirds of them fail in three years or something like that. Incredibly hard work. You've got to have a vision [and be] willing to just invest yourself; and most of them fail. And some of them do great.

This leader was suggesting that in a missional frame the purposes of God precede the strategic intent of human beings. This understanding is not operational among conference constituents.

Conference leaders had met direct and painful anti-missional thinking from their constituents, who assumed that church planting is about replicating the forms of existing congregations. A regional conference minister said, "If a church isn't quite looking the way our established congregation looks, then are they really a church?" At a recent annual meeting of the conference delegates, an emerging church in the new monastic tradition was accepted into conference membership. Though the theological commitments of this church were thoroughly vetted and approved by conference leaders, the executive conference minister related a painful exchange that surfaced during a delegate assembly: "I still shake my head when I recall the first question that came . . . when [we introduced the new church] at annual meeting: 'Why do they want to join us when they are so different than we are?'" Related to the understanding of God's purpose preceding human initiative is the thought that the essence of a church ought to precede its form. This understanding is not widely resident among denominational and conference constituents.

Systemic Confusion

Denominational and conference leaders believed that there is confusion within the system about what missional ecclesiology is and how to put into operation a missional ecclesiology throughout the denomination. A denominational staff person described the state of systemic confusion over what a missional ecclesiology is: "I think that missional ecclesiology and its definition is not resident among various leaders. Be that pastors or others. I think if you asked the question to the person in the pew, one out of a thousand might be able to give you some sort of response."

One regional conference minister said, "We're still defining what it is, so it's hard to think about what changes. We've said we don't want to do things the way we did it ten years ago, but we don't have anything to replace that yet, and it's still in the making." A denominational executive also identified the highly contextual nature of missional ecclesiology as something that confounds the system theoretically and operationally: "Because there are all kinds of contexts and there are going to be all kinds of different models for doing it, in some ways what we need is for the plan to be flexible enough to handle everything, whatever comes along, but still have some ways of doing discernment, or some outlines, that we ask people to minimally fit into."

This systemic confusion operates at several levels. One level of confusion is seen in the diffuse basic assumptions of the organization. Another level of confusion has to do with the struggle to shift from the twentieth-century view of mission as a program of the church to the twenty-first-century missional model of the "church in mission."[2] Finally, there is confusion at the organizational level about how to align the different parts of the church to foster a missional ecclesiology throughout the system.

The state of confusion within Mennonite Church USA about what missional ecclesiology is related to issues of organizational culture as described by Edgar Schein. To understand an organization's culture, one needs "to identify the paradigm by which the members of a group think about, feel about, and judge situations and relationships."[3] Lack of clarity within denominational culture about basic assumptions contributes to a struggle for clarity for top denominational leaders: "Ecclesiology itself

---

2. Ahonen, "Antedating Missional Church," 574.
3. Schein, *Organizational Culture*, 111.

[is the problem]. We are a mix of traditional ecclesiologies . . . that are in operation, which are not in overt operation, but are subliminal things. I am having trouble with *any* kind of definition of, or picture of, missional ecclesiology."

Because of the enormous influence of twentieth-century missionary efforts, the church holds onto a tenacious understanding of mission as a compartmentalized program of the church. There has been ongoing confusion among Mennonite Church USA constituents between *missionary* and *missional*. "That old dedication to the twentieth-century mission [agency] sending [workers] around the world can be understood as an expression of missional church but not the embodiment of it," said a denominational executive. In a follow-up conversation, this person said, "In short, mission is a subset of missional church ecclesiology."

Though there is a declared commitment to missional ecclesiology as the denomination's first priority, at the organizational level, there does not seem to be a clear strategy for aligning the parts of the church to bring this priority into operation throughout the denominational system. The attempt of a denominational executive to characterize the current state of this confusion demonstrated the struggle to articulate what is happening and what needs to be happening:

> Now that we [the denomination] are committed to this, you [parts of the church] figure out what it means in your context. And we've gotten all these contexts and . . . we've got no way to put legs on the verbiage around church-wide commitments . . . that's too categorical . . . not that we have no way . . . we struggle mightily to find ways to put . . . to find church-wide feet under what we say we think we should mean. The other thing—institutions are programmatic which means "doing" and, it's difficult to require institutionally the aspect of missional "being" rather than "doing."

Another denominational executive hinted at a possible but underdeveloped strategy for aligning the parts of the church to bring a missional ecclesiology into operation: "I don't observe that we've created enough of a learning community where conferences are learning from each other. . . . Really, it's not that we all have to be doing the same thing, but we should be . . . encouraging and learning from each other. I don't see a lot of that."

ON CHURCH PLANTING

Denominational and conference leaders were asked to speak to the current state of church planting in Mennonite Church USA. These leaders identified a number of themes, including the lack of a denominational strategy for church planting, confusion over what part of the church is responsible for the goal of developing missional congregations, and current social pressures that may be impacting resistance to church planting. The interview with conference leaders led them to reflect more specifically on the role conference structures might play in a denominational strategy for church planting.

Lack of Strategy

The dominant paradigm for church planting in the past was characterized more by individual initiative than by systemic strategy. An executive director described this phenomenon: "In the recent past decades, church planting seemed to be an individual matter. The phrase was used, 'So and so has a *heart* for church planting.' Therefore they went off and planted a church and so on. So I think we have relied upon individual discretion, which is a hallmark of our understanding of church in Mennonite circles." The elected denominational officer affirmed this characterization, adding an observation that this individualistic approach is lacking in preparation, training, and accountability. Another denominational executive said, "We are in a current stage where there doesn't seem to be a concerted effort in church planting." It was odd to hear a denominational executive reference individual discretion as the hallmark of the understanding of church in Mennonite circles, because corporate discernment is traditionally valued over individual discretion.

Reflecting on the conference's track record with church planting, conference staff members noted their experience of a lack of strategy in a plethora of ways. One staff member suggested that the approach "is not really structured and intentional, like saying, 'We've got to plant so many churches every so many years.'" Another staff member said, "We seem to be relatively unprepared for church plants to arise. We seem not to know how to respond; we don't have procedures for responding to people when they come to us saying that they want to plant a church." A regional conference minister reflected on recent history this way: "It wasn't in anyone's portfolio to work on, and it wasn't a particular priority.

It hasn't been a particular priority of Outreach and Service Committee to work on that end of it. They were okay with dispensing money but tended to say, 'Okay, put an advisory group together and go off and do it, then report back.'"

A conference staff member said, "The [church plants] that have started in the past seven or eight years have all started in a different way and with different structures and unequal funding." A regional conference minister corroborated the denominational leaders' understanding of individual discretion: "It basically started as a vision from a church planter instead of the conference. There hasn't been a consistent plan or structure in place to do it." Another conference minister added, "The observation I've often made is that missions committees would look around and say, 'Here's a city that has a bunch of Mennonites that have moved to it; we ought to start a church there for all these Mennonites that are in town.' I think we've learned along the way that that doesn't work very well because not many of those made it."

A conference staff member summarized the lack of strategy this way: "We've been in a time of transition ever since the inception of the conference. . . . We understood that we weren't going to plant churches the way we used to, but we didn't know *how* we were going to."

Organization Confusion

Denominational leaders identified that the system suffered from a lack of clarity about how each part of the denomination should contribute to the development of missional congregations. A statement by one denominational executive reflected this state of confusion: "It's debated about who and how it's done. . . . Most people feel that it's a good thing to do. Most people don't have an idea how to do it. . . . It is attempted . . . more by church-wide bodies such as conferences and agencies than it appears to be attempted by congregations. In my opinion, it is those bodies that should be encouraging congregations to do that . . . ." Another denominational staff member felt that the situation is even less clear: "We had a kind of denomination-down thrust on church planting. . . . But it doesn't seem to be a focus of denomination-wide activity."

He concluded his remarks by saying, "Some would even wonder if it's an appropriate effort of the church." Denominational leaders suggested that throughout the system one could find ambivalence toward the idea of church planting. This ambivalence was described at the denominational level by one denominational staff member: "Even though there have been declarations made in the past . . . saying that now we are going to have a goal of [church planting] as a church-wide priority, it has been more talk than action." The elected denominational officer reflected on listening to regional constituents' concerns about new church-planting initiatives: "I think when we talk about church planting for some of us coming out of the Midwest, we have a negative response to that because of frequent failure which is a case of gaps in the training and accountability [and] some gaps in the nurturing process. Therefore I sense there's some cynicism: 'Well, there's more money going down a rat hole.' Forgive the crassness."

The other reason cited for this ambivalence has to do with the previously mentioned issues of individualism and acculturation. The denominational leaders shared a perspective that more Mennonite constituents want to be a part of a church that can provide for their felt personal needs and fewer are willing to commit to a new initiative due to fear of what it might require. As one staff member said, "People are less interested in being a part of a church-planting effort. They haven't quite caught a vision for the church that is beyond themselves."

In slight contrast to denominational leaders, conference leaders reflected on the organizational confusion with more urgency. They felt confused about the nature of the role of conference staff within the larger denominational system. There seems to be an intuitive inclination among conference personnel to expect that the denominational leadership will give strategic attention to the development of such a paradigm. The elected conference officer asked in exasperation, "Who presently is in charge?" A conference minister said, "We haven't developed a denominational church-planting strategy and resources [for that]. That's not there. It's up to the conferences to do it." While identifying that conferences need to go ahead and not wait for a roadmap from the denomination, this staff member immediately turned the issue back to denominational leaders: "But are they [denominational leaders] developing models, resources, and structures? I haven't seen that. There doesn't seem to be an overall sense of strategy or model or whatever."

Another staff member wondered if something might be gained if the denominational leadership were simply to allow the strategy to emerge at the conference level: "I think there is something refreshing about each conference wrestling with what it means to plant churches.

I'd have a little bit of concern if Mennonite Church USA would have one structure that all our conferences would be expected to plug into." Yet he concluded his own remarks with less certainty: "On the other hand, it would be nice to have somebody come and help each conference think through how they are doing this. We are kind of on our own, I feel. But I do not want to be handed a plan."

Social Pressure Impacting Church Planting

Beyond the theological and internal organizational issues that pose challenges to developing missional congregations, denominational and conference leaders identified certain social pressures that may negatively impact church-planting initiatives. The first is increasing acculturation that results in a growing ambivalence toward organized religion and a worldview that increasingly reflects postmodern as well as post-Christendom qualities. The second is the current political climate relative to immigration.

Growing acculturation among Mennonites is itself a sign of ambivalence toward the form of church they have known. A denominational executive said that one important role of denominational leadership is to perpetuate and expand a certain understanding of the Christian walk in light of the Anabaptist tradition. He went on to speak of some level of ambivalence among constituents: "We debate about whether [a commitment to the Anabaptist tradition] is a majority position in the Mennonite church anymore. I think that's questionable." Another denominational staff member was concerned that "people are less willing to suggest that faith is something that they want to share with others."

Conference leaders cited social pressures of acculturation within the historic Mennonite culture—largely made up of and led by people of western European descent—as contributing to the complexity of church planting. One conference leader observed, "If the Mennonite church is becoming too easily acculturated to consumerism and the capitalist American society, [the new] groups have a hard time giving their kids role models . . . for living as Christ's alternative community." The immigrant, racial/ethnic groups that are seeking to plant Mennonite churches "are trying to be a part of a church that is already struggling with acculturation."

This leader suggested that the challenges posed by acculturation might also point to an important corrective if traditional Mennonite churches and new immigrant churches were to dialogue together: "In this post-Christian, postmodern society, this very traditional Mennonite church [is] becoming acculturated more than they realize. And so then you have these church plants who . . . sometimes have a keener eye toward where the rest of us are being acculturated, where we might not even realize it. And they might be able to point those things out to us because it gives them *and their youth* problems."

Some aspects of a post-Christendom context include a constellation of divergent values: privatized religion, individualism, new community movements, religious relativism, and a desire for simplicity and clearness.[4] These trends and their corresponding anti-trends suggest that it is no longer possible to talk about an expectation that the world is moving toward Christian normalization. One denominational executive pointed with clarity to this social pressure: "Do I believe that we are part of a larger trend in the North, and particularly following Europe, in which the church is becoming less and less an important part of society? Absolutely. And it's clear among our members, not just society."

Another executive's observations spoke of the weariness people experience with social complexity: "Goodness, life is not getting less complicated with all of us in North American society; our lives are complex; we don't need more complexity." Further conversation on post-Christendom pressures surfaced: "We don't even assume or expect that our commitment to the church is the primary commitment that we carry. It's kind of compartmentalized; it is something that is part of our understanding, but there are all kinds of other things that compete for our time, our attention, and our allegiance."

The realities of globalization and multiculturalism exert pressure on the church's attempts to develop missional congregations across cultures. A denominational staff member's observation suggests that denominational executive leaders, who are largely Anglo, have a steep learning curve in understanding how to address this growing reality: "We [only] flirt with the idea that the church exists for other cultures besides our own. I don't like these explanations, but at any rate, there they are."

Regarding church plants targeted toward specific ethnic enclaves, conference leaders said that immigration issues and language barriers place heavy burdens on the growth and development of new congrega-

---

4. Hempelmann, "Context of Christian Witness," 45–46.

tions. Of these ethnic groups at large, the elected conference officer said, "They are all trying to find room to live in George Bush's new America. For all of the immigrants, especially if they're refugees or undocumented workers, [there is] lots of uncertainty and fear. They're struggling to fit into this wider American pie along with the church pie. You get some of the more White groups [of Mennonites] in a [major metropolitan area within our conference] battering on the walls from the other direction saying, 'There's something more than mainstream America to being in God's realm.'"

People who join the church from various ethnic groups face enormous challenges as they attempt to be true to new spiritual commitments while maintaining relationships with relatives. "The ethnic congregations in particular struggle with generational changes, particularly with language, where the older folks still want to use the mother tongue and the kids are trying to become acculturated as fast as they can." A regional conference minister pointed to the increased challenges immigrants have faced since September 11: "You get a group and think things are finally turning a corner, and the next thing you know they're all gone because there's a raid in the community."

CHURCH PLANTING AND THE ROLE OF CONFERENCE

The conversation with conference leaders around organizational confusion led them to imagine what role the conference might be best positioned to play in a strategy for church planting. As conference leaders began to reflect on their unique role in the denominational system, several things began to happen: (1) they described what they believe they are best positioned to offer in the area of church planting; (2) they described the difficulty of interfacing with those who want to plant churches when there is no pattern in place; and (3) they described qualities necessary for church planters and the struggles that are unique to church planters.

First, because conferences are uniquely positioned between denominational structures and congregations, conference leaders attempt to be highly accessible to congregations and to serve as a key source of assessing what's happening "on the ground" for denominational leaders. These leaders believe that a key contribution they can make in church planting is providing connections. A regional conference minister said, "[Conference] provides connections. I saw the benefit by attending the meeting of [church planters]. It was the first time the church planters came together. . . . It energized them, and they said, 'Finally conference is paying attention to us. We're not a lone ranger out there.' And I think that was important. It connected them to conference in a new kind of way. It communicated to them that conference cared enough about them to bring them together to listen to their story." Another conference minister concurred: "Being able to make connections . . . offers all kinds of different ways of support and probably resources too in terms of people resources and some of those kinds of things. . . . I think that's a key role."

The elected conference officer spoke of the role of making connections to a theological image:

> The comment I was going to make was the connecting that can go on in what is theologically referred to in "body" imagery. Remind these groups that they are not lone rangers out by themselves. That part of connecting is about connecting them with other entities that are somewhat similar to them even if they are quite a distance away. And the other sort of connecting is to connect them with other parts of the Christian community which maybe don't look quite like them. . . . They're part of the larger body of Christ and should be concerned with each other, should be getting acquainted, should be finding ways to support each other whether materially or in other ways.

This conversation on connections led conference leaders to reflect on possible roles they could play in connecting church planters to resources for training and strategy outside the conference in the future. One staff person said, "Conference ought to be providing some tools for church planting. If [we can't] become experts in church planting, then let's develop connections with someone who is and then connect them to these church planters. The relationship is important . . . but then there's also, 'How does one go about this from a practical standpoint? How is one equipped to be a church planter? Where are the models that are out there? What are the skills one needs?' Conference ought to be trying to provide those skills and tools to church planters."

Another conference minister suggested another key role by raising the question of strategy to those who propose to plant churches. Conference ministers are in a unique position to ask key strategic questions: "Is there a plan? Do you have a target? Is this a plan that other churches in the area support?" This conference minister further suggested that conference ministers may be in the position to derail poor planning: "Sometimes somebody needs to say, 'This isn't going to work.'"

Conference leaders made a distinction between conference providing resources and conference connecting church planters to resources. This emphasis surfaced as conference staff members talked about the huge array of resources available. One conference minister said, "We don't need to be resource centers at conference, because churches can go find stuff wherever they want to. All they have to do is get on the Internet, and they've got their fingers in wherever, and so that's a whole other set of dynamics that we haven't quite figured out what to do with or how to work with. [For one church planter] it doesn't matter if it's [one] or [another conference]; he can be in touch with them just as easily as he can be in touch with any of us." The accessibility of training and support tools was seen both as defining the role conference ministers play and as a potential peril where theological differences are concerned.

Second, conference ministry staff members are not sure how to provide leadership when there are no patterns. Since its inception, the conference in this study has not initiated church planting. Of those churches currently being planted, none have originated as a conference-led initiative. Nevertheless, the vision for new congregations continues to develop at the grass roots, in spite of the lack of conference-level strategy. One staff member said, "We seem to be relatively unprepared for church plants to arise. We seem not to know how to respond. We don't have procedures for responding to people when they come to us saying that they want to plant a church." This finds conference leaders scrambling to get ahead of a process that results in unequal resource distribution and attention: "The ones that have started in the past seven or eight years have all started in a different way and with different structures and unequal funding."

Third, conference leaders do have active relationships with those planting churches. They naturally reflected on the qualities they want to see in those who are planting churches. They also identified the places where they see church planters facing unique struggles. A regional conference minister offered, "I think of words like *visionary*, somebody with tenacity, that can dream and see it through . . . passion." In language that reflects clearer missional thinking, one conference leader hoped for "deep faith" and a "commitment to an incarnational ministry, where they believe that the church and Christians are to embody Christ, and in that way meet the needs of the people around them." Reflecting on experiences with church planters, this staff member said, "They are committed to being Anabaptist, theologically Mennonite," yet "they are not limited by old paradigms. Most of them are ready to see the new thing that God might be doing in their community and among their people."

In reflecting on positive qualities for church planters, a regional conference minister hinted at the struggles that are unique to the church-planting experience. This staff member saw a "commitment to a vision . . . in the face of tremendous obstacles." A key struggle for church planters is to figure out how to provide for their livelihood while planting the new church. Another regional conference minister, with past experience as a church planter himself, suggested that church planters need to consider the complexity of being bivocational: "I began by saying church planting is hard work. I think church planting as a bivocational pastor is hard work. Especially when you get above fifty [years old] and your energy isn't what it used to be."

Conference leaders observed that church planters aren't sure how they fit into the rest of the system: "I think they struggle to be understood by other pastors and conference leaders. . . . They struggle to know whether to make their needs known." Other struggles that surfaced included more practical matters, such as money for health insurance and guarding family time, particularly for those who have small children.

5

Iglesia Menonita

In 2003, Raul and Maria Castro moved from the Pacific Northwest to a rural area in the Midwest to plant a Hispanic church in Collegeville, a small city that is home to a major university. Raul had graduated from college and a certificate program in pastoral ministry from seminary, and they had moved to Oregon in 1991 to join the pastoral team in an Anglo church with the intention of starting a new church for a growing Hispanic community. With full-time financial support of local leaders and ongoing advisory support from local pastors who met regularly with him, Raul had been able to plant two churches that continue to thrive.

The vision for a new church in the Midwest began with Carlos, the pastor of a Hispanic Mennonite church in a small city approximately forty miles from the location of the prospective church plant. Carlos had started a Bible study with several families who lived in the prospective city and who traveled forty miles each week to worship at Carlos's church on Sundays. As the Bible study group began to develop an identity, Carlos invited Raul and Maria to move to the area and plant a church for this group.

Carlos told Raul that the area conference provides money for salaries to those who want to plant new churches, although he had not spoken with anyone in conference leadership about the plan to start a new church. After a time of prayer and discernment, Raul and Maria left the Pacific Northwest and moved in with Carlos and his wife until they could find housing.

Raul and Maria came up against three immediate problems. The first was that, unbeknownst to Carlos, a few months prior to the arrival of the Castros, the conference had placed a moratorium on offering salary subsidies to church planters. The second was that the members of the Bible study group that were supposed to be the nucleus of a new church were unwilling to transfer their loyalty from Carlos to Raul. Suddenly Raul and Maria had no income, no place to call home, and no infrastructure to provide guidance. The third problem was that once the couple began meeting with conference leaders and once the intended nucleus for the new church signaled their allegiance, Carlos disengaged from the project.

Prior to his disengagement, Carlos had taken Raul and Maria to meet with a regional conference minister to share their vision for planting a new church. That minister recalled, "They came to my office and shared their vision for starting a new church and [asked] what kind of help there would be available from conference. So I told them I would take their request to the Outreach Committee of conference.... One [thing] we thought important to do was to start a ministry advisory council" to provide local oversight and support for this developing ministry.

Because the intent was to plant a church in the university town, the chairperson of the conference's Outreach Committee invited members of the local Anglo congregation to hear Raul and Maria's vision. After a six-month period of discernment, the Anglo church appointed two members of their church to the ministry advisory committee and agreed to provide space for the new church to worship.

Raul and Maria have been members of the Mennonite church for about thirty years. Those who meet the couple are struck by their warmth and nondefensive demeanor. They inspire trust and are disarming. Though they are originally from Texas, their ancestral roots are in Mexico, and Spanish is their first language. Raul is soft spoken, ever the diplomat. Maria is much more forthright, though not off-putting, in her communication style.

In my interview with Raul, Maria, and members of their ministry advisory committee, the participants recounted the challenges of attempting to plant Iglesia Menonita. Their journey is marked by undying perseverance and fraught with experiences of disappointment and misunderstanding.

After five years of working at developing a new congregation, the Castros do not have a consistent group of worshippers. In my interviews with Raul, Maria, and their conference minister to explore some of the complexities of their experience, six themes emerged: positive missional reflection, anti-missional reflection, systemic confusion, the role of church planter, challenges to progress, and cross-cultural misunderstandings.

POSITIVE MISSIONAL REFLECTION

Participants in this church-planting experiment expressed a common missional understanding that God's mission precedes human initiative. The chairperson of the advisory committee reflected on her sense that God was at work in the broader community:

> I had been shopping at El Baso, the little store on [the highway], and as I was giving them these flyers about this new church starting up, there were also flyers about the Catholic Church starting a Spanish-speaking church. And then much later, sometime this past year, I guess, I found out that the Nazarene church had . . . the same vision at about the same time, and I really have a sense that God was working in different churches to reach out. Now it also was because . . . the census statistics and in the news and everything were showing that there was a growing population.

Other group members talked about human initiative in mission as planting seeds but expecting that God is providing the context in which those seeds grow. One committee member said, "I think seeds are being planted, and we just have to pray and stand beside [Raul and Maria] and wait for God to . . . make the seeds sprout." The conference minister echoed this sentiment, saying, "We do plant the seed, but recognize that it's God who does the growing . . . and so I think that's the theological framework that we operate under."

The participants in the interviews talked clearly about the theological commitments they hold in common. The advisory committee chairperson said, "We are committed to Anabaptist beliefs and theology." The conference minister affirmed Raul's and Maria's theological commitments as consistent with the core beliefs of Mennonite Church USA: "We want this church to be at home in Mennonite Anabaptist theology." These commitments are consistent with a missional perspective that seeks to demonstrate an incarnational ministry.

The chairperson of the advisory committee and the conference minister spoke of the Castros' desire to provide a holistic ministry: "I see Raul and Maria being concerned about the spiritual aspect of people as well as reaching out to meeting human need. You [Raul and Maria] have been outstanding in reaching out to people where the needs are." The advisory committee chairperson concurred: "You're ministering to people that are not being reached out to by other churches, other people, a lot of times, so I think that the ministry advisory council affirms that. Like when you went into Lakeview and shared bread and conversation with people in a very difficult neighborhood. And a lot of churches aren't doing that. Not just because they're not Spanish speakers."

ANTI-MISSIONAL THINKING

In spite of some evidence of missional thinking within this group, there is also a tendency to think in terms of replicating the Castros' past experience of church planting in the Pacific Northwest. This is not surprising, given the financial and advisory support Raul had counted on receiving when he arrived. The formation of the advisory committee itself was a borrowed model. Raul reflected on his previous church-planting experience: "One of the things that we did [in our former community], we started a ministry advisory council. We met once a month and then I did some reporting, had a prayer group just like we're doing here. I think that's one of the things that I requested because that's the experience I had prior."

Though Raul and Maria spent considerable time researching the community in which they were hoping to plant a church, they borrowed a former approach to ministry that did not require them to reside in the context of ministry. Housing in a university city tends to be very expensive, so the couple chose to acquire housing in a town thirty miles away. Raul explained, "Our experience in the past was that we didn't live in the same city where we had the church. We had the church in one town, and we lived in another, and then eventually we moved farther away and still had the church." Maria added, "It wasn't a problem to live in one town and have the church in [another]. That's why, when we came here, we didn't see it as an obstacle. . . . We were not going to make [our home] in Collegeville."

Ministry advisory committee members and other interested constituents had been concerned about the Castros living thirty miles from the context of ministry. The committee chairperson acknowledged that they had asked at a number of points, "Is Collegeville the right place? They always say 'yes,' so then we kind of defer to them and then we might bring it up later, or somebody in the community will ask and I'll bring it to the table again and we'll talk. . . . I have been approached by several people and questioned about why Raul and Maria don't live in Collegeville."

When asked what the group might have done differently in this process, the advisory committee chairperson said, "I would have asked them to live in Collegeville . . . if the ultimate plan is to have a church [there]." Maria responded with a deep sigh, "I'm not going [there]." Because missional ecclesiology is highly contextual, a reliance on what worked in another situation and an unwillingness to consider living in the context of ministry in the current situation is an example of anti-missional thinking.

SYSTEMIC CONFUSION

Raul and Maria landed in the Midwest just as the regional conference was in the midst of a paradigm shift with regard to church planting. During an interview, the conference minister said to Raul and Maria, "You came to us at a time when we're in the middle, in-between plans. We are saying that the previous model that we were following no longer is working. . . . We're in this awkward stage in which we are putting together this model, which will guide us into the future, and it's not together yet." Raul responded, "Well, there is no model." The chairperson of the conference's Outreach Committee said,

> Suddenly there came this request: these people want to plant a church, now what can you do? And that was frustrating . . . because I didn't know what was the right thing to do. It wasn't because of you [Raul and Maria]; it was because of my disconnectedness. And one of the things we needed to do was make several significant decisions about in what ways and how much shall this conference committee help? But our conference committee didn't have the preparations made to make those kinds of decisions yet. We weren't ready for you people to come. And I think the best we can say is that God was pushing us pretty hard to get ready.

REFLECTIONS ON THE ROLE OF THE CHURCH PLANTER

In the midst of systemic confusion, Raul and Maria reflected on their experience as church planters over the previous five years. When asked about his experience in the Midwest, Raul said, "It's been highs and lows.

It's been disheartening, discouraging at times; it's been confusing as well. We thought we knew what God was calling us to do, and as time has gone by, we kind of question him, asking again, 'Did I misunderstand?'" Raul identified a frustrating difference between his former context and the current one: "I didn't have to work full-time; I just concentrated my efforts in church planting, so that was just one difference. Here I'm dividing my time in three or four areas. . . . It's doable, but it takes much longer than when you give your full effort into it."

In spite of disappointment, Raul and Maria both continued to nurture hope for their work. Raul said, "But I feel pretty positive that we didn't make a mistake in coming out [here]. I feel okay about it." Maria concurred: "For me, it's exciting even if we don't have the people right now. You know, we have people sometimes; we do not have people sometimes. But to plant the seed is the most important thing. I told Raul, 'We've been planting, planting, planting, planting. I think the time is coming. People are going to start to show up.' I know [there are] a lot of needs. . . . I feel like sometimes we aren't doing anything, but at the same time somebody calls me to pray for them. . . . We have to be very patient."

As the Castros continued to think back over the previous five years, Raul began to explore his own contribution to the current situation: "I should have been more prepared. And right now I feel that I probably wasn't, or didn't communicate as well as I thought I had." When asked about this, he said, "I feel like I was kind of passive in the conversation. And I [said], 'Okay, whatever,' you know? God called me here so God's going to support me in any way that I need. . . . I think I would have changed my conversation."

Maria reflected on her experience, recalling her initial unwillingness to move to the Midwest: "I wasn't prepared to come here. I was very happy in our former community; I didn't want to leave the church; I didn't want to leave my ministry over there and come here. It was very hard for me because we started all over again." She distinguished her experience from Raul's: "For a man, it's okay. They pack the things and leave. For women, it's another story, you know? . . . For men, it's 'Okay, let's go.' For us, it's very hard. . . . I came because he says the Lord called him, so I have to follow him, right?"

Maria then abruptly said, "But at the same time, I feel happy to do the Lord's work if I have to move. I make peace in my heart. . . . I had to help Raul because it's not only his call, it's my call too. You know, if God called him, God is calling me too to work for him, and even if it is hard, I enjoy doing it too. And I don't think I would ever change this job. I told Raul, if he dies first, believe me, I'm not stopping the ministry." While Maria expressed her reluctance to move, she also expressed her willingness, though it is unclear how her own sense of call balances with her sense of duty.

CHALLENGES TO PROGRESS

The five-year attempt to plant this church had been fraught with challenges. These challenges included lack of time, lack of money, and at times a lack of support from the ministry advisory committee.

The conference minister observed that the lack of time is a frustration shared by Raul, Maria and the ministry advisory committee: "I don't know if it's sadness or frustration with lack of resources, [but] I see Raul and Maria pulled in so many different directions. They have to work in order to live, to eat, and to make their house payments, to pay bills. And I see that as both being in some ways a distraction from starting a church, but at the same time it's in those places of work that they meet people and are involved in ministry."

Raul and Maria were slow to talk about money. Maria said, "We [aren't used to asking] for money, so I feel embarrassed to ask for money. I'm not that kind of person who says, 'Can you help me?' I prefer to get up, go to work, rather than ask for money. I didn't grow up like that." Maria described their situation now, which is quite different from when Raul received a full-time salary: "I saw Raul getting to work a lot in the church. We got involved a lot in the church. We didn't have to get up at five o'clock in the morning, go to work, and come back. I get so tired and I have to go and visit. It's hard, you know? And then when you go to visit in Collegeville, you don't come home at six o'clock. You come home at ten o'clock, eleven sometimes. Then you get up at five o'clock again. You don't sleep a lot." Raul and Maria also cited rising fuel prices as an unforeseen obstacle to trying to establish substantive relationships in a town thirty miles away from where they live.

The Castros find it difficult to express their frustrations over the lack of support they sometimes feel from the advisory committee. Raul said, "I'm very appreciative of the [support we receive], so I have to be careful about what I say, because I like the people."

During the interview with only Raul, Maria, and their conference minister present, they began to speak more specifically to the ways they want to be supported. Raul said, "I need a team of people, three, four, or five people who will commit themselves to help me start this church. Maybe visiting people, people with gifts in music, maybe somebody to help with little kids, for teaching Bible stories, or whatever—just a team to help me." Raul felt that the advisory committee genuinely cares about his ministry, but he said, "[I need them] to be involved more directly, to be a part of this ministry."

Recently, Raul and Maria began meeting in a worship space provided free of charge by a Christian church of another denomination by the river in Collegeville. Last spring, just as a core group of worshippers was beginning to form, the city was ravaged by flooding. The building was flooded, and they lost their worship space. This, of course, was devastating to Raul and Maria, and they were disappointed at the lack of attention advisory committee members paid during that time. "When we opened the church in Collegeville, when it got flooded, nobody came from [the advisory committee].'"

CROSS-CULTURAL MISUNDERSTANDING

Misunderstanding abounds in this case. In the second interview with only the Castros and the conference minister present, the participants were able to begin to describe the nature of this misunderstanding. Their comments fell into three categories: cultural misunderstanding, financial inequity, and ethnic ecclesiastical tribalism.

In the first interview, Raul said during the interview with the advisory committee members present, "I think a lot of what's happened has been cultural. I'm not sure if that's the right phrase or not. Misunderstanding. I think sometimes we talk past each other. Maybe part of it is the culture and language. I try to understand a lot, and sometimes I don't."

The Castros shared more about how they understood the way issues of culture contribute to misunderstanding. Maria said,

> One of the things—maybe you don't understand us or we don't understand you—is that White people—sorry if I call you White people—White people are completely different from Hispanics. It's not easy. What I see in here and in other places where we've lived is that it's not easy to have a church from one day to another one or one month to another one. . . . Sometimes we've faced

expectations like, "You're going to have a church, you're going to start a church, and next year you're supposed to have one hundred people . . . right?" So I hear, "Why don't you have a lot of people; why don't people come?" I don't know why people come and leave. Hispanic people move a lot. . . . They're not happy over here? The next day, they say, "Bye. Good-bye," they're leaving, you know?

The issue of cultural misunderstanding was connected to how the advisory committee and the Castros had related around issues of money. Maria described a poignant example of this confusion:

> One Hispanic pastor received some money because they were students and they had a family. The White church sent a guy to give the money to them . . . and he said, "I came to bring you this money from the church but let's go to the store, because I need to see what you're going to buy." [The Hispanic pastor] said, "You know what? Take your money and go back. I don't need your money."

The Castros related that the requirements of the advisory committee had made them feel that they were not trusted with the money that they received for the support of their work. Raul said,

> I'm very appreciative of the small amounts of support we have received, so I have to be careful for what I say, because I like the people. . . . In talking with our conference minister, . . . sometimes it felt to me like we talked a lot about money, and it made me feel almost like they didn't trust us with money. . . . And I know, I know that we need to do some kind of reporting. For example, in the beginning we went around and around the table whether we needed to report what we did with the money the conference gave. We kind of defined that . . . and then we decided that we didn't have to give a report when the money was used for our living expenses.

The issue of mistrust caused Raul to feel that he was seen as inadequate in the eyes of the advisory committee: "I went to one meeting with our advisory committee, and I feel bad that nothing's happened and conference has paid me money, and I'm sorry. I have to apologize. There have been points throughout that we've felt that, if we had the money, we'd give it back."

The Castros eventually began receiving a small stipend from the conference for their ministry expenses, but they have felt that the conference has not treated them in a way that is financially consistent with others involved in ministry within the conference. Raul reflected on the beginning stages of their ministry in the conference, when they were given the impression by Carlos that the conference would provide a salary for them. Regarding the small stipend Raul received, he said, "I felt uncomfortable with the money that was offered. I said, 'Okay, I'm here, I can't go anywhere. That was the passive side of me. . . . Then I asked a question, 'Well, if somebody else starts a church, are you going to give them [the same money]?'"

The conference minister added another aspect of the financial inequity that the Castros have experienced: "Part of the conference financial support the Castros receive comes on a monthly basis. But it is not always issued in a timely manner. There have been months where they have come to the middle of the month and they haven't gotten a check. . . . Then there's feelings of, 'Well, you don't really respect me; or is it because I am Hispanic?'"

Raul was asked to lead a workshop on immigration issues at the conference's annual delegate assembly. Immigration and undocumented workers had been a politically volatile issue in the Midwest at the time, and some in the audience took issue with Raul's compassion toward undocumented immigrants. Maria found this deeply hurtful: "I don't want to go back to that conference you guys have every year. . . . I left very disappointed with White people. 'What are those immigrants doing here?' And one guy asked Raul in a seminar Raul was leading on ministry to immigrants, 'What are those immigrants doing here? So why are you talking about this, what do you care? If you live here, why do you care?' And I thought [whispering], 'Oh my God, and they say they are *Christians*?' They invited Raul to speak and then asked him why he is living here? I'm very, very disappointed."

The other area that has contributed to misunderstanding has to do with ethnic ecclesiastical tribalism. Raul reflected on his initial meetings with church leaders in the conference, where he felt those in the meetings greeted him with mistrust and skepticism. At one level, he believed this was understandable:

> When I came, nobody knew me. I came out of the blue, I guess. Nobody had the vision except me and Carlos. So I thought the only people who would help me were you guys [local Anglo Mennonite leaders], because you were in the immediate area.

And then I go to this meeting, and I get asked all these questions. After the meeting, I'm left [feeling] abandoned. There was no support. Everybody knew why I was here, but nobody said, "What do you need? How can we help?" Maybe I made a wrong assumption: "I'm a Mennonite; I've been a Mennonite." I know they saw me as Hispanic and probably said, "He's a *Mennonite*?"

Raul and Maria were confused by the cold reception they have received since moving to the Midwest. Raul said, "Well, I was a Mennonite pastor in our former community," I've been a Mennonite there. Started a church. And still, the questions." He continued to reflect on the way his Mennonite identity is not recognized by others: "I've been in the Mennonite church for that long [thirty years]. And consider myself to be a Mennonite. And feel like I [must not be] acting Mennonite; theologically I think I'm Mennonite. Anabaptist. So when I came out here, I didn't come out here as a stranger. But I felt like a stranger. I remember being [bombarded with questions when I arrived here]."

Raul felt that Christians of other traditions have been more receptive than the Mennonite Christians with whom he shares common theological commitments. When the Castros were looking for a place for their church to meet, they were surprised by how long it took the local Anglo Mennonite Church to process their request for worship space to meet on Sunday afternoons. "I was disappointed because I thought I already answered all the questions," Raul said. "And then I asked if I could use somewhere in their building, and it took them six months to decide. I know they probably have a policy."

In contrast, Maria described the experience of requesting meeting space from another Christian church: "When we went to this other church by the river, how long did it take? Maybe a month, two months? No! They said *that day*, 'Come and use our church; we'd love to have you guys. . . . What do you need; how can we help you?' And so, wow! They even went to visit with us in the beginning."

To summarize, Raul offered the following reflection on the overall experience of church planting in the current context: "Well, it's not been easy. . . . It's been difficult, it's been a difficult road, and I just ask myself, 'Where are we going? How can I get there? Or go anywhere?' But it has been difficult . . . frustrating. . . . Hopefully we've been helpful to you."

∼ ∼ ∼

Raul and Maria Castro have been working tirelessly at planting a church in a university city for the past five years while living in a smaller town thirty miles away. Theologically, the church they seek to plant bears some of the marks of a missional ecclesiology. Their primary model for developing the church is their past experience in a West Coast context. Because of the way they were invited to the area, they have encountered significant confusion within the conference system as the conference is developing a new church-planting strategy.

The Castros face ongoing challenges to progress that include lack of time, lack of money, and, at times, a lack of support from the ministry advisory committee. Persistent misunderstanding in the system complicates the development of a cooperative experience with conference leaders and their advisory committee. Aspects of this misunderstanding include cultural misunderstanding, financial inequity, and ethnic ecclesiastical tribalism.

6

Community Mennonite Church

COMMUNITY MENNONITE CHURCH BEGAN meeting for worship on November 5, 2006, in the city of Midtown. The fledging community has been meeting for worship on the first and third Sunday of every month. The members of the core group expect this pattern to continue until the congregation grows to a critical mass of people to carry a fuller schedule of weekly meetings for worship.

I gathered with a group of seven key stakeholders for an evening conversation about their church. The group was made up of three married couples and one married woman whose husband was not able to attend. The participants were all under forty years of age. The lead church planter, Darrell, a seminary graduate, talked about how the vision for Community Mennonite Church emerged:

> The idea came to us as Pete and Mary and we were driving from this area to [our former] Mennonite church [about ninety minutes away]. For Karen and I, it just came up as having kids whom we wanted to grow up in the Mennonite church and with all that meant to us. Realizing that driving more than an hour was not sustainable, and Pete and Mary were also driving [the same distance], it started as a joke: "Hey we ought to start a church or something." With time, that just started to grow, and [was] something I just started to grow with. And Pete, who's a guy who likes to make things happen, also started to run with the idea, and one day we just decided to commit to it.

Darrell, Karen, Pete, and Mary shared their vision with [their former] Mennonite church, where both couples were members, and "they were supportive."

Darrell said that the articulation of the vision for the congregation was largely his work. Since they were a group of two families, he said, "I didn't see the point of putting everyone in the church on a committee to work on the vision. So I wrote one." Darrell's statement, which appears on the back of the church's bulletins for each worship service, reads, "Community Mennonite Church is a member of [the conference] of Mennonite Church USA. Committed to a common life of discipleship under the lordship of Jesus, we meet to worship God and encourage one another in faithful living in a fallen world. Sharing historical values of Anabaptist thought, we seek to apply them in a manner that respects both the individuality of the person and the insight available from one another. We seek to be engaged with the world through practicing Kingdom values in the world."

The vision statement of this new congregation then moves on to a statement of the church's mission: "We seek to enact the Kingdom preached by Jesus in Midtown, through: demonstrating our love of God by loving all people; acting justly and living peaceable lives of nonviolence; practicing reconciliation and demonstrating humility; [and] inviting others to join us in our life of discipleship." Darrell summarized all of this by describing his worldview: "I see a God who changes people and seeks to bring us into an alignment with truth."

Other members of the congregation offered descriptive statements about the emerging nature of this church: "I think one [of our common commitments] is that we are tolerant of everybody's place." Another member said, "I think one of the things we hold in common is a . . . culture of social justice and other kinds of things that go with that that are kind of 'granola' community. So, you know, social justice and environmental issues." One member identified an aspect of the vision that he does not see present but hopes to see in the future. The group hasn't "gone out to do a lot of service work to the community. I think that will come, as we tackle some of the other things in the group."

Community Mennonite Church is being planted in Midtown, a city of 61,000 people in the upper Midwest that is home to a large university. When asked to describe the demographics of the city, the members demonstrated a modest self-consciousness about how their city might be perceived by others. One member summed it up in three words: "White, conservative, America."

Those church members involved on the nearby university campus experience tension between faculty tendencies toward liberal political views and students who reflect a more conservative upbringing. One member who teaches there offered the perspective that the university ethos contrasts in some way with the larger Midtown community: "If you go down to the university, I don't think you have as much of a big C conservative there. In fact, some of my students crab at me about that. I had one student who said of the faculty, 'You're all just liberals, yadda, yadda, [expressing all your liberal outrage] when we went to war with Iraq,' and he just didn't want to hear it."

Another member, who works as a manager in a large manufacturing business, offered this perspective: "In Midtown itself, it's not so much manufacturing as the eastern part of the state. They're more professional [here], if you will, because there are two large hospital systems [in town]. Midtown is the county seat, so there are quite a few professional positions." He said that the city officials have been intentional in shaping the city's workforce. "The industry that [city planners] brought in tends to be a more green, environmentally friendly type of industry than your traditional manufacturing might be. There is also a lot of retail-oriented [business] in Midtown." Another aspect of the context in which this church is being planted is that, as a small city, "it doesn't take long to be in the country. There is still a lot of open farmland and rural [expanse]."

When asked about the religious context of the area, the members were quick to characterize it in stereotypical terms. One member said, "Lutheran, Lutheran, Lutheran . . . Catholic, Catholic, Catholic . . . upper-Midwestern demographics." Another member added, "Throw in a few UCC churches and a couple of Presbyterian, but not much else." When asked about evangelical or contemporary megachurches, one of the participants said, "Well, the evangelicals . . . the Lutherans *are* the Evangelical Lutherans." Karen said that "there are few nondenominational Christian evangelical churches." These, however, were not characterized by the group as megachurches but as "corporate churches." Darrell said, "They're General Baptist, and they work with that [corporate] model."

One aspect of the religious context in which this church is being planted creates confusion about Community Mennonite Church in the community. One member in the congregation said, "There's also some

Old Order, Conservative Mennonites not too far away. So when we tell people 'Mennonite,' they're like, 'Wait, where's your covering?' or 'Are you related to the Weavers at Fall Creek?'" (The Weavers at Fall Creek are known regionally for a store they own and operate that specializes in conservative Mennonite wares.)

One other unique characteristic of the religious context shapes Community Mennonite Church's identity: the meeting place for this new congregation is the only synagogue in town. When approached about Community Mennonite using their space, Temple Sholom "not only agreed, but was excited to rent their worship space to us for Sunday worship." Darrell reflected on this hospitality and the possibility of future interfaith dialogue: "They see the Mennonite experience as similar to their own Jewish experience in that we are both attempting to live lives of peculiar faithfulness within a culture in which we are [often] invisible minorities. They seem excited to teach us how to keep our Sunday fellowship time kosher and willing to provide space and a key." Another member of Community Mennonite reflects on this relationship: "We're attending on a Sunday when other people are not, because of *their* faith."

Community Mennonite Church has developed a strong internal culture in the short time it has existed. This group strives for authenticity in its worship expressions and a semi-formal atmosphere that is not strategically designed to encourage church growth. Darrell said, "We're trying to grow this, and it grows 'as it grows.'" Another member said, "From my perspective, it's a semi-formal group. It still has some formalness to it, due to the structure and repetition that we have each time we meet. But as you can see, we're pretty mellow overall. So if [someone] has an idea that he wants to do something, we say, 'Hey, let's follow through.'"

A significant aspect shaping the culture of this congregation is that the vision originated with two couples who had become Mennonites in adulthood. Yet a number of people who have joined the church have a generations-long Mennonite heritage and happened to relocate to the area. As the focus of the interview moved toward a discussion of the nature of this church, several themes began to emerge, including positive missional reflection, anti-missional reflection, the role of the church planter in developing common understanding among the members, a post-Christendom worldview, and challenges to progress.

POSITIVE MISSIONAL REFLECTION

The participants in the interview did not speak explicitly of a missional ecclesiology. Nevertheless, key missional understandings are foundational to this church's self-understanding. The group reflected a missional ecclesiology in four categories: the preceding mission of God, attention to the intersection of contextual need and the gifts present within the congregation, reaction to modern models of church planting, and the church as self-differentiated from, yet engaged with, the world.

Darrell characterized his understanding of God's mission preceding human initiative. Rather than having a predetermined plan that "mapped" the church's initiative for growth, he hopes for something more organic and in rhythm with God, who is already in motion. "I think there was a relief that [we didn't have a goal that] in eighteen months we should be at X amount and at Y point. . . . [Instead there is a vision] of letting this grow naturally, letting this be what it is today; it is church. We are where we are today, and that's okay. God uses small churches to do his work, he uses poor people to do his work, he uses big churches to do his work."

The understanding of God's preceding mission shapes a value in the congregation for finding where the needs in their context intersect with the gifts God has given the members of Community Mennonite. One member reflected on what she hopes to experience as a member: "For me, it's being a part of a community and providing the community with what the community needs, whether the community is a poor community and they need help building homes, the church would participate in that." Another member reflected on the culture of the church, which seems to invite members to offer the gifts that come most naturally: "Because we're a small group, we kind of elect to do the things we like to do. We have the liberty because we are a small group, so if [people have] an interest in providing snacks every week because [they] like to provide snacks . . . nobody's going to object to it."

There is a strong value for comfort within the group, and as the participants talked about sharing their gifts, it caused one member to share a concern that the comfort level could threaten to turn offering gifts to their context into primarily offering gifts to one another: "I think we tend to be exclusive rather than inclusive, [and] as much as we want to be inclusive, we aren't. And you know, probably as demonstrated by a lot of things that have been said here tonight, we like this church as we're comfortable here. You know, maybe you need to get a little uncomfortable."

The understanding of a missional ecclesiology became clearer as the interview surfaced the group's reaction to modern church-planting models. One member reflecting on the prospect of becoming involved with a new church said it this way: "I thought, *Oh* [long sigh] *church plant, do I want to*? Because I've experienced that, you know, we've got to get the numbers in the door and everybody needs to do this and that and the other thing. This model feels more comfortable." This member's husband concurred:

> Yeah, we're familiar with a church that has to be numbers driven because of financial reasons. And they feel forced to have the followers in order to pay the bills, because of some expansion projects that were taken on without considering the amount of revenue that would be needed to support that. And so, we're not at that point. And I guess from a business standpoint, when you take on additional finances, then you feel like you have to have more people to support those things. And that's when it feels like you're really trying to force people in the door just to accommodate your financial condition.

Another member spoke of her reaction to modern church-planting models when she said, "I don't want to do a *correct* model, I guess. I like and I'm comfortable with this, and I feel like it's the only thing I *can* do right now."

Darrell, the pastor, said, "I went to seminary, which is a [Baptist] seminary." Their model of church planting "does the big launch. The megachurches in the [nearby metropolitan area], most of them are Baptist General Conference. So I sat through those classes and I 'know' how to do it that way, and I was never really comfortable with it." When asked what made him uncomfortable, he said, "I wasn't comfortable with it because it seemed very professional and programmed . . . too, too, almost marketing . . . too sterile . . . too . . . large and 'corporate,' I guess for lack of a better word. I want to reverse that. I want to take the [Scripture] texts that I find so radical and in some ways disturbing and lay that out there as best as I can for people to digest it the best way that they can." Darrell's wife, Karen, added, "I've got a friend who's a church planter, and they just had their 'launch' Sunday, and they've been meeting and planning, getting everything organized and recruiting, and meeting for over a year. And they just launched two weeks ago. That's not who we are."

As the group reflected on modern church models, an underlying cynicism was present, revealed clearly by one member, who said with a hint of sarcasm, "We haven't read *The Purpose Driven Church* yet."

The clearest expression of a missional ecclesiology in this emerging church is a self-understanding of the church as differentiated from society yet engaged with the world. Darrell described the church as a distinct group of people:

> Those of us who are baptized have made a commitment to follow Jesus in discipleship, recognize his authority. Those in the world or in the government don't, and so we seek to model our lives on Jesus and follow the New Testament, and the Bible is authoritative. They [governments] don't. I preached a sermon at seminary two months after September 11 on love of enemy and what would it mean to love Osama bin Laden. What does that mean? I can't believe in locking [him] in a cage for sixty years, I don't know, [sounds] overly loving.

Darrell's seminary classmates were mystified by this message.

Darrell saw Community Mennonite Church's distinctiveness in its being comfortable with itself, unlike other churches: "I see a lot of things that are done that seem to come out of a sense of insecurity with the self, insecurity with being the church, and so there are overreactions one way or another." In contrast, he hopes to be a part of a church that is "comfortable in its own skin . . . not feeling the need to show that it's modern or hip . . . because they're coming from some sort of insecurity . . . that type of confidence that comes from being yourself and not needing to be against anything."

Darrell had recently preached a sermon series on Jonah that challenged his childhood understandings. In looking at the story through a missional lens, he realized that "God called Jonah to preach to his national enemies, the superpower to the north. He faced nationalism, you know. I would say he was a good patriot when he . . . tried to run away to Tarshish. That's extremely relevant out of something that, until I sat down and read it, I mostly thought about as a children's story with a big fish."

While he affirmed witnessing to the state, Darrell is very uncomfortable with modern church approaches to witness that adopt methods from coercive forms of power. He gave an example of a formative experience that oriented him toward methods that are more aligned with the church's message. This is at the heart of his understanding of a missional church that is self-differentiated from, yet engaged with, society.

> I sat back in the eighties and early nineties, and [watched] the way abortion was fought by some groups. In my mind, that was in a lot of ways crossing the line by calling people terrible names and fire-bombing buildings. When you set up a clinic for women who are in crisis, who are in a really tough spot, you can *serve* them. And maybe you provide an alternative witness, an alternative way, and alternative options, and you serve that woman where she is. In my mind, that type of work does more, you know, saves more babies than all the fire-bombing or protests or calling people names or throwing blood or what have you.

As Darrell talked about his "two-kingdom" convictions during the interview, the group listened intently. Hearing him share engaged the group in a way that suggests that the members of the congregation had not spent a lot of time articulating their vision in an overtly missional frame but would like to. One member said, "It would be good for us to have a whole discussion about this. I'm just thinking if we could have this in Sunday school or something about [how all these ideas contribute to] this whole Mennonite church as missional church. How do we use some of the traditional things of what it means to be Mennonites and Anabaptist? How does that contribute to the framework of missional church?"

ANTI-MISSIONAL REFLECTION

Reflecting on things that caused members to join this new church surfaced some anti-missional thinking that is resident among them. Two closely related categories of anti-missional thinking are the allure of replicating past church experiences and a tacit hope for ecclesiastical tribalism.

Among members of the group are individuals who had been involved in Mennonite churches over their lifetime and came to Community Mennonite seeking to replicate a church experience that parallels what they had known in the past. One member, a former Lutheran married to a long-time Mennonite said, "We've been looking for a Mennonite church that was conducive to [my wife's] desire from her background, and we were not able to find that in the number of places we lived, and

[we] coincidentally found Community. And it's exactly what we were looking for." Another member said, "That's one reason why I feel comfortable with this group, because [it's] so much the way [our last congregation] was, and so when I started participating, it was like [sigh] they're talking about the things I like talking about."

One member spoke of an immediate affinity with the worship experience, describing it as "a traditional Mennonite format, which was so comfortable to come back to. . . . I didn't know what to expect, but I came in and it felt comfortable, it felt familiar, it felt like home, you know, it was what I grew up with, it was the Scripture reading and the singing and the sermon and the children's story. It was all there, all the parts." Another member said, "It felt an awful lot like . . . a Mennonite church that we had come from, and the first Sunday we walked in, it immediately felt familiar and comfortable."

Reflecting on starting a church, one member said, "It seems like there ought to be more resources out there for people looking for church. We lived [on the other side of the state] for nine years, and we kept saying, 'You know there really ought to be a Mennonite church over here.' I have a feeling that there were Mennonites there, but I contacted two different conference ministers, asking if they had resources or steps we could take to locate Mennonites. I mean, we were to the point of, 'Should we put in a classified ad looking for Mennonites to attend Bible study?' We didn't know what to do when we were in a non-Mennonite area."

Listening to one another in the interview caused the group to talk about this tendency toward the familiar and making connections with those who are already Mennonite, what I call ecclesiastical tribalism. The impetus for Mennonites to seek one another out when living in an area where there are no Mennonite churches is understandable, given the strong Mennonite cultural identity that persists. A group such as Community Mennonite that is made up of a balanced combination of lifelong Mennonites and people new to the Mennonite faith raises interesting questions about the things that contribute to an authentic Mennonite identity.

One member reflected on this dynamic: "The *Mennonite Weekly Review* had an interesting article [asking] how do we still be Mennonite but expand and not lose that Mennonite identity that says, 'This is who we are because of who we've been for generations'? How do we make the new, first generation of Mennonites comfortable within that six generations of Mennonite institution?"

Another long-time Mennonite member pushed the question further: "How do we open up enough for other people to be comfortable? [My husband] was saying that this group is enough diverse that maybe we will find that we'll have a successful church plant here because there's that bridge between this, you know, hundred-year Mennonite and . . . the 'neo-Mennonite.'" The label "neo-Mennonite" elicited great laughter from the group, and all agreed they had coined a new term.

It is noteworthy that those in the group who raised the question of how to "open" the group to others were not among the originating members of the church. There seemed to be an assumption on the part of lifelong Mennonites that they were demonstrating hospitality to those who preceded them in the formation of the congregation but not in the tradition.

DEVELOPING COMMON UNDERSTANDING

The representatives from Community Mennonite Church reflected on the role and function of the church planter in the developing life and mission of the church, which surfaced three categories: the importance of reflecting in and on action, the need for vision transference between church planter and congregations, and advice to those who want to plant churches.

Darrell reflected on his experience as a church planter with humility and forthright clarity: "I'm the accidental seminarian. People ask, 'Why did you go to seminary?' I was bored; I was working nights and I was bored, so I started taking classes and after a while I thought, 'Well, I guess I better graduate.' And then we were kind of comfortable in the [metro area]. So when we moved to Midtown, I kind of fell into the church-planting thing."

At the time of our conversation, after two years as a licensed minister Darrell was facing the prospect of ordination. "As we were discussing [my] ordination last Sunday, I said, 'I'm here as long as I'm physically able to be here. I'm here until, until at the very least, you can call a full-time pastor.' And then I'll have to decide if I want to be considered for that full-time position. I did not grow up wanting to be a pastor, never felt that's a big part of who I have to be in order to be comfortable with who I am." Though Darrell does not believe being a pastor is important to his own identity, neither does he expect to be far from church work in the years ahead. His hope to lead the church to new horizons is evident in this reflection: "By the time I'm laid in the ground—around eighty-five, so in the next fifty years or so—I'd like to see about four or five Anabaptist churches in the area. So, if we're talking about my vision long term, that would be it. There's no reason why there shouldn't be five churches around here."

Darrell asked an important question of those who would plant churches: "Would you do it even if there would never be a paycheck for you?" He earns his income as a mental-health professional working nights in a metro-area hospital and also owns a small farm near town. He offered an agrarian metaphor for his understanding of vocation: "I garden. I don't make any money gardening. I do it anyway. What type of people do we need doing church planting? It would be those who would just want to do it . . . have a passion for it."

Darrell demonstrated a clear view of seminary education, saying, "I don't like seeing seminary as some[where] you go to get a professional criteria to do X, Y, or Z. It should be a calling to a certain place, and that shouldn't matter if you're working five days during the week." He spoke of his belief that the quality of a church's life should be dependent on something other than the pastor's performance: "You know what? The people you're worshipping with are going to be okay . . . if you spend a little bit too much time hanging onto the text of your sermon and aren't able to just free-flow or walk about like you might want to. Everybody understands."

Darrell said that separating his role as church planter from his livelihood frees him to be a more effective and authentic leader. "I don't want to be market-driven. I don't want to be forced to say something or preach a certain way because that gets the numbers, that's what the most recent trend is in churches that are bringing people, what's the newest gimmick that gets them through the door?" Inspired by an essay by Eugene Peterson entitled "The Subversive Spirituality," Darrell is seeking a role as church planter that is "conscious enough . . . to feel the pulse" of the congregation so that

> if I'm a part of that comfortableness, [I] can take a two- or three-year perspective to subversively inoculate against it. There are times when a congregation, in order to grow, just needs a new voice and new leadership, and maybe that would be the case. But I would hope I would be aware of it and at least be able to take a two- or three-year period to get to the point where the congrega-

tion could make a conscious thought about where they wanted to go in the future. If you want to stay forty-five and happy, great, God can use a perpetually forty-five-member congregation for one hundred years. Or maybe they should come out of that and decide to go in a different direction.

To Darrell, it is critically important to reflect on what is happening in the church as a determiner of his role as church planter and pastor.

Meeting twice each month for worship and socially in-between slows the process of developing a common understanding of the nature of the church among the members. Darrell recalled a recent conversation among church members: "We were talking just last Sunday, and I was asked if I had a timeline on where this Community Mennonite Church should be [by] when . . . and we haven't really sat down with everyone and talked vision." He elicited peals of laughter from the group by saying, "We've kind of put the vision together because we believed we needed something on the bulletin." One member responded wryly, "We need to go on a retreat." Karen said, "At home, [turning to Darrell] I don't know if you want this public, but at home he has said some of this. And I've asked him, 'What happens if we get too big?' And Darrell just [says], 'Well, I'll start another one in [the closest city].'"

Though the group had not spent much time talking about their common understandings about the nature of the church that is being planted, they demonstrated a lot of trust in Darrell's leadership and comfort with the way he articulates vision for the congregation, including the vision statement. A member of the church described the vision statement as a "living document," indicating that the church members do not feel excluded from becoming involved in shaping that vision as they wish. On the other hand, it isn't clear how much of the comfort level with the current stated vision has to do with the tacit agreements shared among some members about what a Mennonite church is.

When asked about advice they would give to conference and denominational leaders with regard to church planting, Darrell and members of the church offered two ideas. One member, who works in business management, asked, "Do they have a startup committee or a planning committee or even, you know, call 1-800—so you can contact a person who is a resource for church plants? [Is there] a resource to go to and say, 'We would like to do this. What are some steps we need to make this a successful startup?' And it wouldn't need to be financial . . . just a resource for structure and startup."

Another member wondered about a role for someone at another level of church to be thinking about the qualitative way that new churches originate: "Something that pops into my mind is [to ask], 'Is that church somehow coming up naturally?' What I'm hearing is we're kind of a natural progression [that] wasn't forced in any way. These others, were they being forced to pick a spot on the map and put a church here? Is there a difference in how this is coming about?"

A POST-CHRISTENDOM WORLDVIEW

Most participants in Community Mennonite Church described the context in which the church is being planted in stereotypical terms. At a gathering of church planters in April 2008, Darrell characterized his context by saying, "We are planting a church in Christendom." However, the worldview of Community Mennonite seems to stand in contrast to this context. Participants in the interview reflected a post-Christendom worldview in two ways: ambivalence toward modern expressions of church and the search for belonging.

A newcomer to Community Mennonite offered the following insight on her spiritual pilgrimage. In her reflection, one hears a desire for spiritual connection that is not confined to modern denominational loyalties.

> My background and my husband's . . . it's been a trial time for us. . . . We want something for our children, but we're not sure where we stand, especially my husband. . . . He knows where he stands, but it's not wholeheartedly in any church. . . . Oh, I think [of] the Catholic churches in our area . . . and I haven't tried them all out for my family. But the one I grew up in, because I'm from here . . . I've had some fights with it. I think you have to look for a church that's 80-20, and if you're really disgusted about 80 percent, then you can't go there. So I like parts of the church I grew up in and went to as a teenager, and I just haven't shopped around to the other ones because I think they're going to be less in another area. . . . So it depends what you're looking for.

This participant also spoke of the spiritual quest of post-Christendom society as an individual journey: "This is where I'm from, this is where I am right now, and this is where I hope to be."

Other participants in the group talked about the failure of modern expressions of church to offer constructive guidance. There is a sense that the spiritual guidance offered by the modern church is characterized by reductionism and is overly simplistic. One member said, "I'm really not comfortable with a book called [something like] Twelve Steps to Christian Maturity.... No, it was even worse than that, it was like Twelve Days... it wasn't even Twelve Steps [everyone laughs]... That makes me feel physically ill when I see something like that." The same participant also spoke of the "three-point sermon to a great marriage. I've known many people who are married for fifty years and tried a lot of different three steps, so I would say, let's talk about other things, let's talk about commitment and slogging through together."

As group members talked about their disillusionment with modern expressions of church, they began to describe what they were looking for from the church. "It's not so much, how are you, are you doing daily devotions? It's not that," one member said. "It's more, are we living in a way that gives a witness to our beliefs?" The desire has more to do with finding companions for a journey than seeking a vendor of therapeutic services.

Participants at Community Mennonite Church illustrated the trend/anti-trend impulse of postmodern individuals seeking an experience of community that validates their individuality. One member spoke of hoping to belong to a church that is "pretty laid back. Not a lot of pressure... not a lot of expectation to participate if you choose not to. I've experienced it as 'come as you are, be what you are.'"

Some participants at Community Mennonite are finding a place of belonging that is starting to feel like home. One member recalled what another member, recently returned from vacation, said at a recent gathering: "He commented during the service that when they stepped in the door, it felt like home... that it was not a passing phase... that it was 'yes,' this is where they belonged." But for another member, that sense of belonging is still a way off: "For me, it's becoming a community, but it's still not like you're going home.... It's not 'going home' for me yet.... When I go to Catholic church, I'm like, 'Oh, yeah, right... this is where, for so long, that feels good.' But the songs at our church are becoming more a part of who I am. But it can't happen overnight when you've done umpteen years of something else."

CHALLENGES TO PROGRESS

The participants in this interview were unanimous in their desire to let their church grow naturally. They placed very few expectations on themselves for a particular rate of growth. The major challenge to progress identified within the group is related to a post-Christendom sense of commitment to organized religion. Most group members confessed to a level of commitment that makes participation less than top priority. One member said, "We visited the first Sunday we lived here but then couldn't get our act together until last fall to attend." Another member held back commitment out of fear that becoming involved in a church plant might ask more of her than she could give: "Did we want to be in the forefront or hidden behind? You never know with a church plant if it's going to be 'go out and beat the bushes for membership,' or taking it one step at a time."

A lifelong Mennonite in the group talked about the quandary of growing disillusionment with her involvement in a mainline Protestant congregation:

> We had been plugged into [that church] but were becoming increasingly disenfranchised there for a variety of reasons that I won't go into. And I knew the Mennonite church was meeting in Midtown, but because we had plugged into [that church], had not really thought about pulling the kids out of a church where they were plugged in, where they were attending Sunday school, where they had friends, [to attend] the Mennonite church. But [we] decided to at least visit, and so we've been attending as often as we can make it, which is not every other Sunday [though we hope to].

Community Mennonite Church is in the formative stages of becoming a congregation. It is a collection mostly of young-adult couples with children who embrace a post-Christendom worldview in the midst of a broader religious context that largely reflects Christendom values. The intent to offer an alternative expression of church is one of the most striking aspects of this church.

Community Mennonite demonstrates a number of missional and anti-missional attributes, most of which remain largely tacit. The church planter, Darrell, reflects deeply on his role as leader and vision developer.

He demonstrates a clear reproducing rather than replicating vision for this church. His dream, shared by others in the group, is for Community Mennonite to become a hub of multiplying congregations in the area. Darrell recognizes the need to have a more intentional conversation with the congregation about common theological commitments. Members of the church would welcome such conversation and do not feel disempowered by the absence of these conversations. They recognize that there are many commitments that are assumed because of the lifelong Mennonites in the group.

It remains to be seen what will happen to the common commitments of the congregation if the lifelong Mennonites continue to view themselves as "hosting neo-Mennonites" into the Mennonite tradition, particularly for "neo-Mennonites" whose theological commitments are overt rather than assumed and whose investment precedes involvement of lifelong Mennonites in this local congregation.

7

New Covenant Hmong Mennonite Church

BECAUSE OF THEIR COLLABORATION with the American CIA during the Vietnam War, the Hmong became the target of persecution after the war. They fled Vietnam and spent many years in refugee camps in Laos and Thailand before being resettled in other countries around the world. Approximately 60,000 Hmong people live in a major metropolitan area in the upper Midwest. Many of these people found their way to the area between 1990 and 1992 because of the state's refugee-friendly policies. The Hmong people also perceive that this metropolitan area offers better job opportunities than many other places in the United States.

New Covenant Hmong Mennonite Church began there in January 2004. Because the group had no building, its first worship service was held in the home of church planter Foua Lee, with four families present. By April of the same year, the church began renting space from another church. New Covenant became an official member of the Midwest Mennonite conference in July 2004. In 2007, a celebration marked the church's transition to an independent, self-supporting church.

Worship in this church is conducted in a mixture of two, and sometimes more, languages. Pastor Foua said it is important for English to be spoken in the worship services in addition to the Hmong language to retain a connection with the youth of the church. By 2007, the worshipping community of New Covenant was made up of sixteen families consisting of eighty-seven people. The "tag line" of the church reads, "Together we worship God, seek truth and walk humbly with our God." Foua reported that about 70 percent of the members joined the church as new Christians. About 30 percent had a Christian background before coming to the church but had stopped attending their former church.

Leaders in the church suggested that the Hmong people moved to the area because of the economic opportunities it offered. Hmong people prefer to be self-employed as small-business owners, a goal many have been able to realize in this urban area. The Hmong culture is made up of only eighteen clans. Marriages are often arranged, and marrying within one's clan is not allowed. The culture places a high value on intergenerational support. Upon marrying, couples are expected to move into the home of the husband's parents. According to Foua, because the Hmong people began coming to America as refugees just twenty years ago, many of the older generation "have no education, no job, and there is a lot of poverty."

In 1994, Foua was living in Fresno, California, and was sent by his church to a denominational college to attend a two-year pastoral ministry program. Upon completion of that degree, he returned to California and was a pastor in Fresno for three years. In 1999, he moved to Colorado to be a pastor for youth in the Hmong Mennonite Church in Denver. In 2003, Foua was asked to move in order to plant churches in the upper Midwest.

From the beginning, Foua and those who sent him anticipated the planting of multiple Mennonite churches in the area. Shortly before he arrived, the founding leader of the Hmong Mennonite Church in the United States approached leaders of the conference with a proposal for the new church plant and suggested ways the conference could be helpful. Conference leaders created a reference council to provide relational support for this new work.

To understand the nature of New Covenant Hmong Mennonite Church, I conducted an interview at a gathering of the church's key leaders. Members of a reference council appointed by the conference to provide support and counsel for the fledgling church were also present for the interview. A follow-up interview was conducted with the pastor and another lay leader after the congregation celebrated becoming a self-supporting church in 2007.

The interviews surfaced a number of themes that spoke to the nature of the church that is being planted. These themes are all nuanced by the centralized role the church planter plays in the development of this new Hmong congregation. They included the church planter's role in the origination and deployment of a vision, positive missional reflection, the church planter's role in developing common theological commitments within the church community, and the church planter's role in developing leadership for ministry. The interviews also surfaced some perceived challenges to progress.

VISION ORIGINATION AND DEPLOYMENT

As members recounted the story of New Covenant Hmong Mennonite Church, the prominence of the church planter's role in the development of the new church became apparent. The church planter was appointed by the founding member of the first Hmong Mennonite church in the United States in consultation with other influential leaders. Though the responsibility for the vision of this church lies primarily with the church planter, development of shared ownership of the vision has required Foua to be both relational and strategic.

Foua reflected on how the vision for the new church originated and developed in a way that suggests that this work is his to shape. Members of the Anglo reference council expressed their willingness to trust his intuition, wisdom and judgment. One member of the reference council said, "I agree with Foua that the vision [primarily falls] on the church planter. . . . I view us as a support agent to connect with conference and hopefully to bridge [the] gap and build community" between the Hmong church and other conference congregations. Another member of the reference council demonstrated humility in his desire to learn from a Hmong leader: "I think success to me in this work is the fact that they're teaching me. . . . I feel as if I've been a believer the majority of my life and I've tried to do God's will, and it's a humbling experience to see new believers bring something to you that can really impact you, and I needed to be humbled."

According to Foua, in Hmong church culture, "only the pastor or church planter is in charge of the goal." He said, "In my vision, Foua starts this church. I have dreamed of bringing Hmong people to come to know God . . . and in my vision for this work, I want to see it grow and make paths into this community. It is not what the church name is or who we are, but because of who we worship. Who Jesus Christ is and whose kingdom we are of. This is my vision for planting a church among the Hmong people."

Foua's approach to church planting is highly relational and strategic. His ministry is based on making individual contacts. One of the biggest influences in Hmong culture is the traditional animist religious practices involving shamanism, with its heavy reliance on the clan leader. When planting churches, Foua's strategy of evangelism is to build relationships with individuals and then attempt to reach the clan leader. Foua said, "When a family converts to Christianity, the clan leader will convince them to be non-Christian again, so it is very difficult. . . .We are attempting to approach the leader first. This is more difficult and takes a lot of time." Foua has found that when a clan leader converts to Christianity, many of the other clan members follow.

POSITIVE MISSIONAL REFLECTION

Though he was not explicit about his understanding of missional ecclesiology, when asked about the role of missional ecclesiology in his work, Foua expressed appreciation for a missional way of framing the church. He suggested that missional ecclesiology is an understanding that provides a useful bridge for common vision among Mennonite leaders across cultures. Foua commented that when he meets with his Anglo Mennonite colleagues for monthly meetings, he shares much in common with the ecclesiology he hears them describe.

Foua is self-conscious that the language barrier that causes him to be slow to speak may make it appear to others that he is not in agreement with what is being described. Aspects of a missional ecclesiology are evident as he talks about the church as itself commissioned, the incarnational emphasis of his theology, the importance of allowing context to shape ministry, and the importance of hospitality as a spiritual discipline.

First, Foua identified a foundational commitment to the missional understanding of the church as itself sent. The mission posted on the church's website quotes the Great Commission: "All authority in heaven and on earth has been given to me. Go therefore and make disciples of all nations, baptizing them in the name of the Father and of the Son and of the Holy Spirit, and teaching them to obey everything that I have commanded you. And remember, I am with you always, to the end of the age" (Matt 28:18–20). The church's mission statement is explicit in its understanding that all of the church has been sent to go and make disciples: "New Covenant Hmong Mennonite Church believes that Jesus commissions and commands all Christians. We are called to spread the Gospel of Christ."

Second, Foua strives to develop an incarnational, or cruciform, ministry within his congregation. Being a missional church, "we teach the gospel and train leaders in the way Jesus came . . . so we encourage our people to live like Jesus' teaching." In speaking to the needs of people, Foua's intent is for his church not only to speak good news but also to be an expression of good news. This was most evident as he expressed his vision for the church to confront the violence that has been a historic characteristic of his culture:

> My vision is to lead this church to a position of nonresistance. For example, in our history, the Hmong lived in several countries, surviving by means of violence. But when we know Christ, we become Christians, and we want everybody to become Christians. We want them to live a peaceful life, to love each other. No more fighting. No more war. We want everyone to be baptized, to be saved. . . . We are to live in community and love each other and help each other. This is the way we want to be the church.

Third, Foua expressed concern that a strategy for church planting pay careful attention to the missional impulse of contextualization. His counsel to anyone developing a strategy of church planting was to pay special attention to the ethnic context in which that church is being planted. He believed that the people best equipped to plant a church among a particular ethnic group are those who share that same ethnic heritage.

> I would tell them to find the church planter for any group who would plant a church. For example, if you want to plant a church among the Vietnamese, the church planter should know about Vietnamese culture or Vietnamese language, or should know Vietnamese background. Also, if you want to plant a Mexican church, the church planter should be someone who understands the Mexican people. But a Mexican person should not be asked to plant among Vietnamese. Or Vietnamese cannot plant among Mexican. Or, for example, a Hmong church planter who knows Hmong culture, the Hmong language, this is who should plant churches among Hmong people.

Foua hoped to develop a ministry that is highly sensitive to contextual needs.

The fourth aspect of missional ecclesiology is the expression of hospitality as a spiritual discipline. One leader of New Covenant characterized the quality of relationships within the church this way: "The nature of the church that Pastor Foua has planted . . . feels really close, like a family. And I think that's how it's supposed to feel. Everyone knows everyone else personally. If anyone needs anything, it's just a phone call away." Foua affirmed the strength of this quality but also challenged it: "For the congregation, right now, we have fellowship, but next I will change fellowship to hospitality. We need to visit, go house to house, to bring people together. So I think I need to change the ministry [from the past] to the future."

DEVELOPING COMMON UNDERSTANDING

When asked about the common theological commitments of the New Covenant Hmong Mennonite Church, Foua wanted to make sure that he was understood, so he wrote the foundational commitments down and passed them out as he answered this question. He described the theological commitments of his church this way: "We hold a covenant, the idea of a religious community based on the New Testament model. The Sermon on the Mount informs our core beliefs and we believe that this agrees with the Anabaptist tradition. We believe in the authority of Scripture and the Holy Spirit and salvation, and we practice believers baptism, and we do discipleship, and we practice discipline in the church. We practice communion, remembrance of Jesus in the breaking of bread. We believe in nonviolence and we do not swear oaths."

When asked how he develops common understanding for these theological concepts within his congregation, Foua cited the importance of his role as teacher: "I have to explain my vision for the church. I will lead this group to the vision we set forth. Everyone has to know the vision. I have to preach or teach the vision every three months to remind them of the vision and tell them to remember the vision where we are."

When asked if he experiences resistance to his theological commitments, Foua said, "Yes, sometimes people have a different idea, a different vision. Someone may 'vote' against me, but it's very important to talk with the people who criticize the vision. We need to have some step to stand on." Here Foua was referring to the need to compare foundational commitments when there are differences of opinion. "We try to find [out] why this person disagrees with my vision, and I have to find out

why he criticizes me, and so I try to aim my vision a little bit higher....
I try to lead them. I have to try to make them understand."

Foua offered an example of resistance and his willingness to allow latitude in his principles: "I had one family [who] came to church. They decided to be baptized right away. And I think about people who have been baptized [in] the way we have baptized people in the past. We provide instruction prior to baptism or we have a class for those who want to be baptized, but they decided immediately to convert and be baptized. So this happened to me one time. And it really surprised me, but I baptized them, then I trained and taught them; I had a class for them afterward."

Foua also illuminated a key cultural understanding of effective leadership with regard to developing common understanding in the community: "In Hmong culture, to be a good leader, the leader has to be first, and willing to do by action, not by word. People see you do the right thing and they respect you. So as leader you have to do it first. If they see you going the right direction, then they believe you, they follow you, they respect you." In Foua's cultural tradition, leadership roles may be conferred, but authority to lead is always earned.

LEADERSHIP DEVELOPMENT

Given the centrality of the church planter's role within Hmong culture, one might think there would be a tendency to marginalize the leadership development of others in the group. On the contrary, leadership development is one of the most intentional initiatives of Foua's leadership. One of the most striking things in the interview was the presence of the lay leaders from New Covenant Hmong Mennonite Church. Foua brought the church council chairperson, the treasurer, the youth leader, and the secretary. All these leaders were young professional people under the age of thirty.

During a planning meeting of the church leaders and reference council, the lay leaders were unself-conscious and deeply engaged in answering the questions of reference council members and explaining the strategic operations of the church. When they were unsure of how to respond, they looked to Foua at the end of the table, and he would provide a brief answer, prompting the others to continue. Otherwise Foua remained silent.

For the taped interview, the roles reversed, and the lay leaders offered fewer contributions to the conversation, deferring to Foua as spokesman for the group. His approach to leadership development appears to be characterized by sharing the leadership platform, formal training experiences, and developing a worldview of the church as self-differentiated from the world.

Members of the Anglo reference council spoke enthusiastically about Foua's work in developing leaders in the church. One member of the council observed, "Foua isn't doing everything like other ministers, [feeling] that they have to do everything themselves. . . . One of the important things is that he's working with the young people, even the teenagers, and getting them involved in the worship service as well." Another reference council member added, "That is something that Foua has done since the start. . . . He doesn't set himself up on a pedestal. He works directly with and supports and encourages his members" to become leaders. One church member said, "I agree that we constantly involve a lot of activity at church to develop a lot of leadership for everybody individually, so that is the strength I see for the church."

In another encounter with New Covenant Hmong Mennonite Church, I was present for a formal leadership training workshop led by the founding leader of the Hmong Mennonite Church in the United States. Fifteen young adults gathered in an unfinished basement of a home to spend the entire day receiving leadership training. In conversation during a break, a young woman was asked why she had come. She responded, "Well, I just decided, if I was going to be a leader in this church, I had better learn how to be a good one. So I am here to receive whatever help I can to be a good leader for the church."

A specific task in leadership development seems to be the cultivation of a worldview that trusts the wisdom of the church more than the wisdom of the world. Foua said, "We have to know good or bad advice in this work. So we want to question, where are we getting our advice from? From God, from the Word, or the world, or from people who are working against God's work in this world. So . . . we need to be very careful about when advice comes from some people who are against God's work."

Reflecting on the proclivity for violence in Hmong culture, a young adult member said, "Being a leader, there are a lot of people that would do what they can to take you down . . . give you false advice. They would ask a lot of wrong questions to discourage you and just ask questions to bring you down, from teenagers to older people as well. So I think that is one of the greatest threats to discourage us. I pray to God every day to be with each and every one of us, especially the leaders."

CHALLENGES TO PROGRESS

The participants in the interview identified a number of signs that the church was developing and gaining in strength. One reference council member said, "Starting a new church anywhere, among any group of people, is a very difficult task these days, and the fact that we have a congregation of [more than] sixty people in three years is a sign of something positive." Yet the leaders of the church and members of the Anglo reference council spent a large part of the time during the interview talking about the things they perceive to be challenges to progress. These challenges were expressed in terms of the cultural pressures, language barrier, finances, and facility.

As stated earlier, because the majority of the Hmong people continue in animist religious practices, clan leaders and families place tremendous pressure on those who convert to Christianity. This causes many individuals who convert to practice their new faith or retain their old practices in covert ways. One young adult leader in the church said, "We have a lot of elders who carry old traditions, nonbelievers, so for a new church to have any members you have to break the barrier and 'make' them into a believer. So it's kind of hard for a Hmong person to do that. So first you start small and with relatives, then you grow from there. Once you convert them to believe 100 percent, the hard part is to break the barrier to make them a believer." In a follow-up conversation, this leader wanted to be clear that he was not suggesting that conversion needs to be coerced, only that those who take a step away from traditional religious practices experience tremendous pressure to return, and it seems that only as they make a complete break from their tradition can they grow in their faith as Christians.

Language barriers pose another challenge to progress. While most young people in Hmong culture are encouraged to learn English as soon and as quickly as possible, many of the community elders do not speak English and rely on their children and grandchildren when navigating the English-speaking world. This language barrier slows understanding between Foua and the Anglo reference council members who seek to offer support. One reference council member said that, after four years of working together, "I understand a little bit more each time we meet. Foua and others tell me a little bit about Hmong culture and Hmong community and things that work in the Hmong community. And that is part of catching up, you know, and maybe we were too arrogant going in." Language barriers also create confusion within the congregation. Foua said, "Yes, other languages, our young generation, they don't know Hmong language, so I have to speak in English and Hmong and mix together the languages. And sometimes I need to speak in the Laos and Thai language also."

The language barrier also slows the process of training. Many training materials available to Foua are written only in English. Reading these materials is difficult in itself for him, but only after reading a resource can he evaluate whether it is even useful or relevant for his culture. "I read some articles a couple of times that did not fit for Hmong culture," he said. "They might have been useful for people of other cultures. I see some resources like that."

Foua and his leaders identified finances as a challenge to making progress. In traditional Hmong culture, shamans do not earn their livelihood from their work as spiritual leaders. While Hmong people bring money or animals for religious ceremonies, they do not easily understand the need to provide financial support for the operations of their churches and the salaries of their pastors. "There's a lack of financial support," Foua said. "They believe that we leaders are satisfied, so it looks like we don't need financial support for the congregation." Foua said financial issues are a point where Anglo leaders do not understand Hmong experience. "They don't consider that poverty is a problem. In Anglo culture, I see the support of the church; they provide financial support to the congregation so they can stand financially strong. I see it a little bit different from the Hmong people."

Finally, members of New Covenant Hmong Mennonite Church long for a facility of their own. Since the beginning, the church has rented space from other churches. This means that their worship services must be scheduled when the facility is not in use by the owners. Typically, the church gathers for worship in the middle of the afternoon. Real estate in the area is prohibitively expensive, and so the prospect of owning their own space feels like a distant hope.

Nevertheless, congregational leaders see owning their own building as an important element in the New Covenant's continued growth. One young leader in Foua's church said, "I think definitely having our own building, to have more flexibility and to do what [we] want to do is important. We have to rush constantly, every service, to get it over on time before the next group starts their service. So that is the main reason I think if we had our own building, we would have more time to do our preaching and more time to plan, so I think that is a key issue."

New Covenant Hmong Mennonite Church has been in existence for six years. This church was planted by a leader who was appointed by influential Hmong leaders. It has developed a formal relationship with a regional conference through a cooperative relationship between the church planter and an Anglo reference council.

The central role of the church planter shapes the strategy of the church's development. Pastor Foua sees himself as the primary bearer of the church's vision. He demonstrates an awareness and appreciation for a missional ecclesiology. He sees the roles of preacher and teacher as the key media by which common understanding develops within the church. Foua is deeply committed to the task of leadership development through sharing the leadership platform, formal training experiences, and instilling a worldview of self-differentiation from the world. New Covenant Hmong Mennonite Church also faces a number of challenges to progress that include cultural pressures, language barriers, finances, and facility.

8

Hospitality House

Hospitality House was started in 2004 by Michael and Angie, who "gathered a handful of friends together and started a church in [a densely populated neighborhood in a Midwestern metropolitan area]." The church grew to about fifty people, few of whom live in the neighborhood. "Most of the people lived in the 'burbs, hung out in the 'burbs, and only came to the neighborhood for a Sunday gathering." Out of frustration, Michael and Angie "went back to the drawing board . . . a few times." Their church's website says, "Out of the ashes of what once was, a new Hospitality House emerged—a community anchored in the neighborhood and centered on Jesus' way of peace, hospitality, simplicity, and prayer."

The neighborhood "is a diverse neighborhood of immigrants, refugees, punks, artists, homeless people, students, activists, and professionals," according to the church's website. It exists within one square mile. It is, in fact, the most densely populated square mile between Chicago and Los Angeles, containing close to nine thousand economically diverse residents. More than two-thirds of the neighborhood is low-income or below the poverty level. Besides Hospitality House, there is currently only one other Christian Ministry present in the neighborhood: a church-sponsored coffee shop.

The community life of Hospitality House centers around two households in which some of the members choose to live. The synergy of Anabaptist theology that Michael was exposed to in seminary with recurrent Anabaptist themes in the new monastic movement caused him to seek a relationship with the regional conference of Mennonite Church USA. His vision to instill an Anabaptist identity is seen in the name of the first community house acquired for the church, Sattler House, named after an early Anabaptist martyr. In June of 2008, Hospitality House was accepted into formal membership in the conference.

Formal affiliation with Mennonite Church USA does not limit the vision of Hospitality House to the relational network of a single denomination. A community house named for an Anabaptist martyr and a newly acquired community house, Clare House, named in honor of St. Clare of Assisi, is illustrative of a deep hope for the unity of the whole church. Michael further demonstrates this vision for church-wide unity in his coordination of an active ecumenical web-based community.

Michael continues to be a key leader in the developing network of new monastic communities around the world. His connection to this network is nurtured through an active web-based ministry that includes a website for networking among church leaders who want to have conversation about Anabaptism and new monasticism. Michael also produces a web-based magazine. The website is a clearinghouse for "propaganda meant to frustrate and disrupt quaint notions of Jesus, and even quainter notions of the religion he founded. . . . But beyond disruption and subversion, we want to proclaim something much deeper: hope. You can only change things for so long before you need to help create the alternative. . . . We want to captivate [people] with a kingdom vision and explore what it would look like to make that a tangible reality."

In the tradition of new monasticism, Hospitality House has developed a "rule" for common life. The preamble of this rule says, "Hospitality House is committed to Jesus' way of peace, simplicity, prayer and hospitality. Hospitality House lives to embody Jesus' presence—particularly in this neighborhood. Members of Hospitality House commit themselves to three things: centering their lives on Jesus Christ, being present to the neighborhood, and sharing their lives with one another."

The members of this community center their lives on Jesus Christ through careful reading of the Gospels in a dialectic that moves from gospel to life and life to gospel. The community has published its own breviary to guide community members in their morning and evening prayers. Hospitality House strives to be present to people on the edges of society. The members also seek to live a life of humility and modesty in contrast to an affluent society. The members of Hospitality House agree to forsake violence in all its forms and instead to seek and promote peaceful ways of resolving conflict.

The members of the community are present to the neighborhood by "spending time understanding the cultures of the neighborhood through the intentional building of friendship," as the community's "rule" says. They remember the people of the neighborhood in their daily prayers. They extend hospitality to their neighbors, "sharing what they have with those in need, whether it is a simple meal, clothing, a place to sleep for the night, or . . . friendship."

Members of Hospitality House build a common life together by seeking "the living and active person of Jesus Christ" in their brothers and sisters. They commit to regular attendance at Hospitality House's gatherings. Intercessory prayer for one another, material sharing, and the pursuit of reconciliation are all named values intended to guide the deepening of a shared common life. The rhythms that foster common life include a Sunday evening gathering at Clare House to eat together, pray, engage the Scriptures, discuss, and sing. On Wednesday evening, the community gathers at Sattler House for an open meal for the people of the community and their guests. Following the meal, the community prays together.

On Saturdays from noon until 4:00 p.m., the community participates in what has come to be known as the Hospitality Train. They load up their bike trailers with fresh ingredients and high-quality cooking equipment to feed people good food at a vacant lot in the neighborhood. Occasionally musicians come and play while the meal is being served. It has become a place where the diverse segments of the neighborhood gather. It has also caused them to come under the scrutiny of Homeland Security officials during a national political convention held nearby.

Michael, Angie, and two other key leaders of Hospitality House invited me to share in the community's Wednesday evening meal, and I conducted an interview with Michael, Angie and the other two leaders afterward. I approached Sattler House, a modest bungalow set amid many blocks of similar story-and-a-half homes that appear to have been built in the 1920s. The yards are clearly sized to use the land to maximum effect. I was welcomed into the house as the table was being set for supper. A group of about twenty people was gathered in the living area, talking and laughing easily, waiting for others to arrive. The group was made up of young adults, all under forty years of age. Four small children were playing among the adults. There were several married couples, but the majority were single. I was struck by their easy and comfortable manner with one another. As they became aware that I had entered the house, several came, one at a time, and welcomed me, asking my name and offering theirs and then returning to the living-area conversation.

A cooking snafu at Clare House caused one carload of people to delay the meal more than an hour. No one seemed concerned about schedule, so when all the food had arrived, it was set on the table. The food was a healthy array of fresh vegetables and pasta. Following the meal, I met with the key leaders, whom Michael had identified for the interview, in a common living space on the second floor.

These leaders of Hospitality House reflected deeply on their experience, and a number of themes emerged, including positive missional reflection, reflections on the role of church planter in developing common understanding within the community, a post-Christendom worldview, and challenges to progress.

POSITIVE MISSIONAL REFLECTION

It is clear from the interview with the Hospitality House leaders that a missional ecclesiology has been foundational from the church's beginning. They described a missional ecclesiology in five categories: the preceding mission of God; hospitality; reactions to modern church understanding; the church as self-differentiated from but engaged with the world; and a desire for incarnational ministry.

The leaders of Hospitality House spoke directly of an understanding of God's mission preceding human initiative. Angie stated that the name for the church was chosen because they "really wanted to see where God was at work in the neighborhood" when they first moved there. She added, "None of the people who were involved in the planning . . . had any real background in that neighborhood, so we really wanted to see where God was at work, kind of submit ourselves to the neighborhood, and that is what we've tried to do in various ways over the course of our existence."

This attention to God's preceding mission resulted in the church's decision to dovetail with existing initiatives in the community. Angie said, "So instead of starting with an ESL [English as a Second Language] course or program, we volunteered at one, and now I teach ESL at one of the programs locally. Instead of starting our own [bike] cooperative, John works on bikes and builds bikes at an existing bike cooperative." Church leaders spoke of trying to learn from the neighborhood and then asking God to show them where God is working and where God wants them to get involved.

The leaders of Hospitality House spoke often of hospitality as a foundational core value that shapes the ministry of their congregation. Carla said, "One of the things that really defined the church *is* hospitality." Another leader said, "One of the main things that identifies our community is hospitality, so we try to just have an invitational attitude. People may need a place to stay for transitional housing or a place to stay for the night . . . but [we also want to include] people that we've known for only a day or two or that a friend of ours might recommend."

It is hard to grasp the lengths to which hospitality is extended by this group. A young man, newly released from prison and in need of transitional housing, occupied the main level bedroom and was present at the Wednesday evening meal. One leader said, "We try to always have an open room." Hospitality offered at table fellowship is also extended to the neighborhood. Michael said, "We have two weekly meals, one in our home and one outside, so that even the one outside is not trying to feed the homeless people, or something like that. It's trying to build community, just trying to have a meal for everybody so that everybody that's around on the sidewalk, walking past, would feel welcome to come and stay and talk and just participate." Hospitality House members intentionally serve the meal with crockery table service and silverware so that those who come to eat will stay and fellowship rather than walk away with disposable plates and utensils.

Church planters Michael and Angie tie the ideas of God's preceding mission and hospitality together as a single issue. Hospitality for this church is not only something offered but also something received. When asked for advice that he might give someone wanting to plant a church, Michael said, "Before you plant a church . . . you need to submit to the neighborhood for a while first. So ideally, someone should just work and live and hang out in the neighborhood for at least a year before they even start doing anything tangible as far as ministry . . . so they are really . . . understanding where they are."

Michael said he prefers this approach to what has been traditionally termed "urban ministry." He described the traditional approach to urban ministry as the "White man's burden": "'We're all well-educated White people going into a brown neighborhood and saving them all.' There's so many problems with that." Michael and Angie spoke of hospitality in terms of receiving the hospitality of their context as a way of earning the trust of their neighborhood. After four years of living in the neighborhood, Michael said, "I think we're still learning."

The clarity of vision for a missional ecclesiology among the leaders of Hospitality House is also evident in their reactions against modern church patterns that limit the common life of many modern worshipping communities to Sunday morning worship and midweek programming. John, a key leader in the congregation, said, "We've tried to build something that works outside the boundaries of just one weekly gathering. Church for us isn't contained in the walls of one single structure." One gets the sense of a more organic understanding of what church is and how it happens. He continued, "Any time any of us are getting together, even if it's as simple as over coffee at the local coffee shop, we're together. We try to be really commonly focused on community things. Then church is what happens whenever we're together, any of us. So we try to include or bring that idea of the church into all areas of our life rather than compartmentalizing events and that sort of thing."

Michael said that results are a secondary concern to attention given to the quality of their common life. Results are often understood only in retrospect: "I stop and look at what most churches do in general, even if they have a lot of resources . . . and then [when I] think, 'Well, it's just a handful of us,' it's really amazing."

While the leaders of Hospitality House root their missional ecclesiology in God's preceding mission and in being received by and engaged with the community, the identity of their church is self-differentiated from mainstream society. Michael said, "I like to think we've created a culture where we look at some things, especially what Jesus said, and not let ourselves get off the hook about what we're supposed to do about it, but always keep those awkward, challenging things of Jesus in front of us and then let our life together be a way of always grappling with this to figure out how to live them together." Michael saw this pursuit as a contrast to mainstream society: "Part of this process is [giving ourselves] permission to be really awkward." In addition to being seen as awkward, Michael hoped that his community will shun a "high production value," so there is room "to take risks and fail and be awkward."

John suggested that, while the church is engaged with the neighborhood, the call of the church is from one kind of lifestyle to another: "Wherever the starting point, we're always trying to invite each other into the community and the community rhythms." Angie hopes that Hospitality House will increasingly reflect the faces of their neighborhood and that people will "put up their own houses to use for this purpose." She was realistic about the challenges of relating to a large immigrant population in the neighborhood: "In large part, the immigrant population is transitional, and very likely, as they can, they will be moving to other parts of the city or other parts of the state or nation. But it would be nice to be able to have our hospitality include more of the span of the neighborhood population."

A final commitment to missional ecclesiology is related to the issue of incarnational ministry. Though the leaders identified the explicit value of hospitality, they had also been on a steep learning curve to understand how that value is embodied. John's wife, Carla, a native of Peru, was confessional about this struggle: "My heart wants to do what God wants me to do, and I want to bring hospitality, and I want to share with people." Yet she told of a critical incident that challenged her resolve: "As a mom, I remember back one or two years ago, we had our first son, Mateo, and we lived in this house, and we were opening the house for people that would need a place to stay, whether we would know them or not. And I got really scared. I got a baby, what's going to happen?"

The leaders reflected openly about that experience and how they processed it. The incident involved a homeless man who had been kicked out of his treatment program. He had "done it in a way that was not trustworthy, and so it was a question, 'How much can we trust this guy we kind of know, but do we really?'" Upon being turned away, the man became drunk and disorderly to the point that he was taken to jail for the night. Michael referred to this as "the first really risky hospitality event," and it made them question "how do we actually do this . . . how do we do it in a safe way?"

This incident was a painful learning experience for the community. Michael said, "I know you guys [John and Carla] talked about 'Do we even fit here?' That was also a time when I felt like throwing it in. But it was hard to be mad about it, because . . . who else do I know, what other mom with children do I know, that's going to put up with strangers in the house?" Michael insisted that the group make the decision together, because "what's the point of adopting someone into the family if you can't respect the family that they're being adopted into. So everybody had to agree. And so to me, that was a moment where . . . hospitality could [no longer] be abstract."

Though John and Carla ultimately decided to move into an apartment in a neighborhood cooperative, the result of the discernment process confirmed her commitment to the vision of Hospitality House: "The vision that Hospitality House has is the same vision that John and I have. I think that God put the plan in our lives that we want to do this, we want to be family for people that need family. Whether we know them or not. Whether they seem reliable. Whether they seem to be fine or not."

Reflecting on this experience, John said, "I think that created some healthy opportunities, because the house can be a house of hospitality now and we can remain involved . . . both as individuals and also as a collective community while keeping all these boundaries that are appropriate for all of our lives and the church." Michael concurred that this event was formative: "Now we're at a better place, so we have things differentiated. John and Carla are involved. Maybe not [in] housing, but they are involved in the hospitality process. Everyone can have a different part in the process and not everyone has to have the same role. That's a hard thing to learn. And we had to figure it out together. And how do kids affect that? What level of the [community] house does John really have? All sorts of things had to be figured out together."

Having resolved the issue of hospitality at one level, Michael anticipated further struggles on the horizon as the community strives to become more incarnational in ministry. There are many systemic pressures on the stability of the neighborhood. Michael said that there may be a role for the community to play in confronting the powers of institutional planners who want to deconstruct the neighborhood and disburse the immigrant population as a "political" answer to the Somali youth violence that abounds in the neighborhood. "Once we start talking about protest and people getting arrested . . . ," he said, "people are going to get uncomfortable. . . . John and Jared got picked up for dumpster diving. And there's this family in the community that are older, and they commute [from the suburbs], and the father of the family is upset a little bit."

DEVELOPING COMMON UNDERSTANDING

During the interview, the leaders of Hospitality House reflected on the role and function of the church planter in the experience of this church. These reflections surfaced three categories: the ability to reflect honestly and humbly on experience, the role of the church planter in fostering common theological commitments within the community, and the way common understanding develops in the community of the church's mission.

The leaders of Hospitality House agreed that Michael is the church planter, founder, and originator of vision for Hospitality House. However he demonstrates a self-effacing leadership style that is confessional and humble. He reflects deeply on his experiences. Reviewing initial attempts to start the church, Michael said, "We were trying to just gather some people for a weekly gathering. . . . And we put that idea to death and really made it about relationship and discipleship and living a way of life together. We got really small really fast. It's only been in the last two years that we started having some consistency and were able to build."

There were times when Michael thought about quitting: "Yeah, the big one was when we . . . were using this as a community house, and we had a number of people living with us that were helpers and a number of people living with us that were in need of hospitality, so they took relational resources. And for some reason, not sure, I can't remember who it was, but we had a number of people all leave at once, except for the needy people, and Angie and I almost fried out."

Michael also recalled an episode that brought him closest to quitting: "This sounds boastful, but I was at this place where I was wondering if I had any limits, because I'd never experienced them before. And I was finishing seminary, teaching a course at the seminary, throwing a conference on consumerism, coming on staff with InterVarsity, all at the same time. I was driving, and all of a sudden I went hysterical, which was an anti-stress response because I was pushing myself. So I had to get home, I had to get home. I just basically speed-walked home, which was two miles, without even getting tired, because I had all this energy that needed to get burned off."

Having endured these times of hardship, Michael was optimistic about the future of Hospitality House: "Now we're at a point where we have enough people, like I could finally say that if I got shot by an assassin [chuckles], Hospitality House might survive, which has only been in the last few months that I could say that." When asked to describe what success looks like for Hospitality House, Michael said, "To me . . . when I'm twenty years older and looking at what we've done, I'd like to see a number of communities around the country or wherever that have people who were part of our community and learned to do community from Hospitality House." The hope for deploying this vision for church is structured into the fabric of Hospitality House's organization. The church maintains open spaces for short-term and full apprentices to join fully into the community's life for three to nine months as a learning experience.

Michael carefully articulated the theological commitments that are important to him and to which he is calling the church: "One of the things in our community is we don't divide a line between ethics and theology. So simplicity, peacemaking, prayer, and hospitality are shared commitments that really shape how we see the gospel." While it was easy to list these commitments, Michael was careful to anchor them all: "Underneath all that, the bullet point would be, a very Christ-centered ethic as a theological commitment." Michael gave the example of "peacemaking not only as a theological category, but [as] . . . a shared theological commitment. The fact that Christ is actually present in the community, and so at any given point the posture should be discerning what God is doing in our midst . . . everything in Scripture has to be discerned in light of Christ's presence."

John followed up by saying, "It also has to do with the fact that we try not to see doing some sort of service that's abstract from Christ, but instead, we're actually trying to live with Jesus, with him, because we believe that Jesus is creating these things, and doing these things, *and his kingdom exists*, and this is what it looks like. We're trying to live that, we're not trying to just go off and do our own thing because of some sort of belief."

Angie agreed with Michael and John as they talked about the common theological commitments of the church, but she added another dimension that brings further clarity to the commitments of Hospitality House: she saw Michael's web writings as an important way that many people become aware of Hospitality House. So "people that come really understand, . . . are almost able to have the vision before they come here, as they read on the Internet some of the writing and the rule of faith."

It would be easy to believe that a charismatic and articulate leader can attract a group of followers who expect the leader to be the primary bearer of the vision. Leaders at Hospitality House have worked hard to develop common understanding and ownership for the community's mission among all the members. Michael suggested that the central leadership challenge for him was "figuring out how to basically be able to hand things off, even if they could be done better if I just did them myself." John put it in these terms: "We try to foster a communal discernment of our things so most everyone is involved in discussing [and discerning] issues."

For John the evolution of the vision for Hospitality House paralleled the evolution of the community's own development. "Because we've gone four years of an intensifying vision and an intensifying common way of life, and centering things around that, I think we've just kind of cultivated this culture [where] to the extent that you're invested in Hospitality House, your life is invested and committed to it."

Michael emphasized the importance of the clear articulation of the community's rule as people come to explore the church: "The nice thing is that we have a standard [articulated] that we're calling people toward. So if people don't engage as much as somebody else, it's still the same standard we're working toward, so it's still the same rallying point."

Another aspect that contributes to the development of common understanding of the church's vision is that those who join Hospitality House may be a self-selecting population. Angie reflected on this by saying, "There have been people added to the community who were, idea-wise and vision-wise, on the same page and aware of Hospitality House for a while, and so they've come. It's totally different than having people just come and check us out and have their own hopes about what we'd be like. Usually [they're] disappointed because it wasn't whatever they . . . had in mind."

Michael continued by describing the kind of people who come to Hospitality House: "People are going to come for one of two reasons. They're either going to like the ideas, and they're going to get involved and commit to a place. Or they're people that are already in the neighborhood and love the neighborhood and basically [we try] to evangelize them to what we're about." Because the leaders are inviting people to a rule of life, which is a higher standard than most churches have for attendance, people "have to buy into a vision [to the point] that they are invested in it and they can't just be skimming off someone else's vision."

This understanding shaped Michael's view of his own leadership: "What that creates for me is just the task of being like the older brother who helps people live consistently according to the vision as much as they can." This has resulted in an ever-growing common vision "to the extent that people are able to do that [follow the rule] they become co-bearers of the vision."

A POST-CHRISTENDOM WORLDVIEW

As the leaders of Hospitality House shared their story, it became apparent that the model of church they are striving for reflects a post-Christendom worldview. This surfaced in three ways: differentiation from the world, responding to a societal search for belonging, and an ambivalence toward modern and programmatic expressions of church.

Hospitality House is an attempt to do something different, to be an alternative form of church. In their embrace of a missional ecclesiology, they expressed reactive attitudes toward modern and programmatic expressions of church. John said, "For most of the time, we embraced this idea of not being defined by certain events and not having our identity being defined by things like building or an event or very finite things." Michael pointed to an 80-20 principle of church involvement: "If you had one hundred people and 80 percent would kind of attend and 20 percent would do stuff—we didn't want that. And basically we said, 'How can we just build a church with the 20 percent?'" Angie brought this idea back to the concept of God's preceding mission that is "so much less a programmatic type of thing where we start something and plan it . . . and much more trying to participate in what's already going on and see what needs to be added, maybe down the road."

The leaders of Hospitality House are very aware of the fragmentation of an American society torn between individualism and a deep hunger for belonging. Angie said, "Most people live lives that are so spread out and do their shopping all over and their friends are all over and their life is just very spread out. And so we are trying to encourage people to be involved here and cut out some of that and focus more here." It was noted that committing to life in one place cuts against the grain of American individualism. Angie spoke of people who couldn't share the passion for the neighborhood. Nevertheless, Hospitality House leaders open-handedly "encouraged them to focus closer to home, wherever they were."

As has been seen in earlier reflections, the leaders of Hospitality House characterized deep hunger for community as a longing for family. An exchange between Michael and John illustrates this: "There's lots of people involved that we got to know through the neighborhood that in some way or another think of us as their community." John added, "Or family." Michael concluded, "Yeah, family, which to me is more—even though it means that they are less likely to attend but more likely to show up at your house in the middle of the night and want something. So that's the trade-off. More like a family than an institution."

Reflecting on this idea of redefining family as family of faith, Michael said, "The goal should be to live out your faith with a family of people who live out your faith with you and that you're hospitable, and you have a . . . porous boundary of who can be family. That's different than . . . going into the city, into the bad neighborhood and saving it . . . and saving those people from the thing they've created for themselves."

CHALLENGES TO PROGRESS

Throughout the interview, the leaders of Hospitality House highlighted perceived challenges to their progress. These challenges include contextual complexities, ambivalent commitments, and finances.

For all the cultural diversity of the neighborhood, it is not an easy place to do ministry. Michael joked that "God told us the wrong neighborhood because [this] would be easier in almost any other neighborhood in the entire [metro area]. I think the part of it that was my decision—and not God's—just wanted to pick the hardest neighborhood possible to plant a church." The cost of housing makes it difficult for people to think of becoming permanent residents and makes it hard for the church to acquire more community housing. "In this neighborhood . . . the housing is so expensive because there's so many students," Michael said. "What isn't run by the professional management group for a number of large housing cooperatives is divvied up into duplexes or triplexes," and that makes housing pricier.

The neighborhood is home to a series of large, high-rise, cooperative housing projects. Michael spoke about the complexity that such a concentration of cooperative housing poses: "John and Carla live in cooperative housing. You have to meet requirements to live there, so you couldn't have a community house. This makes it hard for us to be an intentional community." The cost of housing was a factor when the "community almost collapsed down to just the five of us and the kids with a few people that were kind of a little bit involved."

Another challenge to progress is ambivalence in commitment when prospective members are confronted with the hard realities of this kind of ministry. Michael reflected on his early naïveté: "I thought I heard so many people talk about the ideal, and we decided to live this ideal. It's not perfect, but most of the people around think it's a big deal. There's just a number of people that can talk a really big talk about the ideal and say they'd jump at the chance to live that way. But really, when you actually get down to it, . . . they say, 'No, I'd rather just not even try . . . but good for you for trying.'"

Michael also reflected on some frustration at the lack of impact other leaders in the new monastic movement have had: "I would have thought [writing by] people like Shane Claiborne would have made our job easier, but it's almost made it harder. They have these naïve expectations of just getting to sit around having deep, heartfelt conversations with perfectly chiseled young men playing drums with dreadlocks, who have winning smiles. We only have one guy that fits that description, and he doesn't have dreadlocks."

One of the big surprises for this community is how "incredibly hard it is to raise funds and support what we are doing," Angie said. "People seem so supportive of what we're doing, but" the financial support doesn't seem to come through. John shared on Michael's behalf that the times he'd come closest to quitting resulted from "frustration over how difficult it is to both raise funds and to get things going, and feeling . . . like there's so many obstacles, that it's just discouraging."

Thinking about the things that threaten to derail Hospitality House led these leaders into reflecting on the advice they would give others trying to do the same thing and also to reflect on the current systems for preparing church planters. Michael said that to be best positioned for this type of church planting, someone should have a "really flexible, decent-paying job that allows you to do this and the time to get money from it." John suggested that someone attempting to plant churches should welcome the risk and the learning opportunities that failure provides: "Don't be afraid to screw up at all, like we've just gone through years and years of realizing that we're screwing up left and right. . . . You just can't be afraid to get your hands dirty."

Michael also said that there is much that could be improved in the traditional educational models found in seminaries:

> When some people ask me, and they're around the age of twenty or younger, I tell them, if this [type of church planting] is something you want to do, then you shouldn't take the career ministry route of education, which equals a lot of data and not a lot of helpful training. Not to brag on John, but I always feel like if I could bring him to these seminary classes . . . people wouldn't think he's not a seminary student, and even though he's not gone to college or gotten any formal training of any sort, he's been saturated.

Michael added, "You know it's the practical skills you'll need. For most seminaries, even their urban ministries [training] is inadequate because they're still assuming you're coming into an existing two-hundred-member congregation that has certain kinds of programmatic approaches to urban ministry."

So, what would the leaders of Hospitality House recommend as a proper training path? Michael suggested that the best training program would include "some kind of vo-tech education for two years and then two more years of some sort of neighborhood development curriculum." He has a high view of the church as theological training ground: "We can handle the theological training here." This seems to be consistent with church as conceived by anyone labeled "new monastic." While it is hard to argue with the effectiveness of the church-based theological training that Hospitality House has been able to do, it has been in large part due to Michael's ability to be an effective translator of his formal seminary education to his base community.

As the interview came to a close, Michael's parting words to me seem to symbolize the breadth of all that was shared: "I hope you enjoy your long trip home. I mean, I'm tired and you look tired. We have a spare bedroom if you want to spend the night."

Hospitality House emerged as an intentional community whose life centers on two community houses that a number of members share. Other members live in private homes but are deeply involved in the corporate life of the church. The current membership of the church consists of approximately thirty adults and several small children. The church members commit themselves to a "rule" of living as an alternative society marked by worship, prayer, hospitality, and reconciliation. It involves a church planter who is seeking to develop a new church in the "new monastic" model.

While being realistic about the possibility that there is a gap between Mennonite theology and Mennonite reality, the church planter, Michael, sought a fraternal relationship with the Mennonite conference leaders, "seeking the wisdom of the lived tradition." He is representative of a new generation of church leaders who are disillusioned with Christendom models of church. Though this church has officially become a member of Mennonite Church USA, Michael works hard at developing a web-based community of like-minded church leaders across the country from many Christian traditions as well as an active web-based magazine that provides a forum for developing new understandings of the church in the face of Christendom's demise.

Part 3

Conclusions

Having listened to the stories in part 2, we will now begin to look at them in light of the four research questions my study posed. As we do, we will better understanding how relationships, behaviors, and organization within a denominational structure either support or fail to support the development of missional congregations; how new churches best align with a missional ecclesiology; how church planters and their stakeholders contend with contextual pressures; and how church planters perceive their roles.

In chapter 9, following a description of the cases, an analysis of the interviews will answer the four research questions of my study and provide insight into possible solutions. Chapter 10 will report the major findings as well as recommendations to bring clarity to the process of church planting in Mennonite Church USA. I hope that the analyses, insights, findings, and recommendations in these chapters will be useful to other denominational and church-planting leaders as well.

9

Cross-Case Analysis

THE VISION FOR ALL four of the church plants whose stories were told in part 2 originated outside any conference or denominational initiative to plant them. In fact, three of the four plants emerged just as the conference had declared a moratorium on the prior model of church planting and before conference leaders were able to articulate a new strategy for church planting. These churches were born in the crucible of complex social contexts and a denominational system in the midst of arrested organizational change.

Allow me to quickly summarize the results of the analysis of interviews, documents, and observations: Ten distinct themes surfaced across the cases: (1) underdeveloped missional culture within the denominational system, (2) lack of structural alignment to support a missional ecclesiology within the denominational system, (3) common theological commitments, (4) positive missional reflection, (5) anti-missional reflection, (6) cultural and social pressures, (7) post-Christendom worldviews, (8) challenges to progress, (9) the church planter's role in developing common understanding among key stakeholders, and (10) leadership development.

These themes can be grouped into four broader areas, each speaking to one of the four research questions (listed in this book's introduction): (1) cultural and structural issues within the denominational system (themes 1–2); (2) theological commitments and missional ecclesiology (themes 3–5); (3) contextual pressures with which church planters contend as they seek to plant churches (themes 6–8), and (4) the church planter's role relative to the nature of the church that is being planted (themes 9–10). We will explore these themes as a response to their related question.

QUESTION 1: STRUCTURAL AND ORGANIZATIONAL ISSUES

Again, the problem explored in my study is the confusion church planters and their key stakeholders experience at a time when denominational and conference leaders of Mennonite Church USA are struggling to reconcile the discrepancy between a stated mission and current performance.

Five years into the creation of this denomination, the delegates of the denomination's general assembly adopted a mission statement which, in part, envisions "developing and nurturing missional congregations of many cultures." Two years later, following a six-year review process, the Executive Board of Mennonite Church USA, speaking with "a single and unified voice," reported to the constituency of the denomination "that our vision and call to engage in God's purposes in the world is not adequately supported by our present relationships, behaviors and organization."[1]

The first question investigated this discrepancy between stated mission and underperformance: "In what ways do the relationships, behaviors, and organization of Mennonite Church USA support or fail to support the development of 'missional congregations' within Mennonite Church USA and one Midwestern regional conference?" Two subthemes emerged in the interviews that demonstrate the "relationships, behaviors, and organization" that do not support developing missional congregations of many cultures: an underdeveloped missional culture within the organization and inadequate structural alignment of the denomination.

Underdeveloped Missional Culture

Placing missional ecclesiology as the centerpiece of the new denomination's culture represented a significant shift in organizational culture. However, the organizational culture of Mennonite Church USA is not sufficiently developed to carry the freight of planting missional congregations of many cultures. As the Executive Board pronounced, the relationships, behaviors, and organization of Mennonite Church USA do not adequately support the denomination's mission.

The interview responses from denominational and conference leaders showed that a missional ecclesiology has not become operational

---

1. Houser, "Executive Board to Strengthen," 22.

Cross-Case Analysis 113

at the level of organizational culture because it is too far out of line with the organization's prior assumptions. Five prior assumptions seem to be disrupting the process of implementing a missional ecclesiology as the foundation for developing missional congregations through the denominational system.

1. Denominational and conference leaders identified the struggle to make the paradigm shift from the past-century model of "mission as program of the church" to the emerging model of "church in mission."

2. Denominational and conference leaders believe that the denomination functions with multiple ecclesiologies borrowed from many traditions that are largely tacit, making it difficult to agree on strategy.

3. Church planting in the past had largely been seen as something that happens as an initiative of an individual who "has a heart for church planting." Thinking about a denominational or conference strategy for church planting requires something new of the denominational structure and the self-understanding of denominational and conference leaders.

4. Denominational and conference leaders believe that there is some level of ambivalence toward church planting among the constituents of Mennonite Church USA. This may be due to past experiences of church plants that failed to thrive or a reaction to the past-century model of church planting that seemed intent on colonizing neighborhoods.

5. A prevailing assumption from prior models of church planting assumes that new churches will be built by gathering the "lost sons and daughters of Menno" living in urban centers. In other words, there is an assumption that Mennonites living in an urban area would prefer to attend a Mennonite church if the option were available to them.

What is more perplexing about the current situation is the lack of planning for developing missional congregations at the levels of structure, strategy, and process. There seems to be a resignation on the part of denominational and conference leaders that a strategy for church planting is really about something or someone else in the system. For example, some in the denomination believe that church planting is best initiated by individuals "who have a heart for it"; therefore it has little to do with denominational or conference strategy. Ambivalence among constituents of Mennonite Church USA toward the idea of church planting raises the question of whether leaders believe that a denominational strategy for church planting would receive enough support from the constituency to justify the investment.

Finally, the persistent notion that the preferred method of church development is to gather Mennonites who have relocated to urban areas seems to be the method that emerges in a strategic vacuum. The members of Community Mennonite Church were most explicit in expecting that someone somewhere in the denominational system keep track of where Mennonites move so that they could be invited to participate in the development of a new church. For longtime Mennonites at Community Mennonite, this seemed to be the preferred method for growth. This assumption is neither proven effective nor missional.

It is understandable that Mennonite Church USA would struggle in making the transition in its organizational culture from "church with a mission" to "church in mission." Many denominations are struggling to make this transition. The persistence of prior assumptions is due in large part to how influential Western missionary activity was in the past century. There is a natural resistance to developing a new organizational culture that dismantles the way mission has been framed, the way mission is assessed, and how congregations at the grass roots understand their role in mission relative to local, regional, and denominational bodies.

It is also understandable that, given the power of religious broadcasting and the absence of an established or "favored" national church, American Christianity would become a great melting pot of many ecclesiologies resident among the constituents of any one denomination. Because these ecclesiologies are largely unstated, it is normal to expect them to be at work in unconscious ways among those who hold them. It is incumbent on the denominational staff (from here on referred to as Executive Leadership) to give concerted effort to the clear articulation of a missional ecclesiology within an Anabaptist theological framework.

Denominational and conference leaders of Mennonite Church USA tend to look primarily through the structural and political frames. They may do well to consider how a missional ecclesiology is affected when the denominational system is viewed through the human resources and symbolic frames.

Using the human resources frame, denominational and conference leaders might gain the nimble and flexible organization they want by scanning the environment for those who are already doing the work that aligns with the stated mission. This might open spaces for denominational and conference leaders to develop new forms of partnership that are more effective than traditional "in-house" programmatic structures. This could result in a better "fit" between the organization and the stated mission than "forcing" the current staff to become competent in areas where they have little or no experience.

On the other hand, using the symbolic frame, denominational and conference leaders might focus on metaphor and ritual, opening spaces for denominational and conference leaders to communicate the ambiguities of a missional ecclesiology more effectively to constituents who have understood mission in more "instrumental" terms. In instrumental terms, the question of appropriate strategy is often framed in terms of accountable results. This is a question not well matched to the enterprise of church planting, which can rarely be distilled to cause and effect. In the symbolic frame, the question shifts from "results" to "meaning." From "What has been accomplished?" to "What is expressed? What is attracted? and What is legitimized?"[2] These questions seem well matched to a missional ecclesiology that is concerned about contextual relevance and reciprocating hospitality.

Inadequate Structural Alignment

The structure of the denominational system is not adequately aligned to put into operation a missional ecclesiology among denominational and conference leaders relative to developing congregations of many cultures. Mennonite Church USA is in the midst of an evolutionary change. As mentioned earlier in the book, evolutionary change can be considered a two-stage process. The first stage is intended to be a relatively short period in which organizational leaders make large changes in the organization system. This is followed by a longer period of convergence in which leaders effect smaller changes, intending to align the parts of the system to the broader strategic mission.

---

2. Bolman and Deal, *Reframing Organizations*, 249.

While the intent to be missional signaled a period of reorientation, the period of convergence that was intended to follow appears to have stalled, resulting in a lack of structural alignment. Participants in this study identified three issues of structural alignment that impede church planting in Mennonite Church USA.

First, denominational, conference, and church-planting leaders agree that there is considerable confusion about how each part of the denomination should contribute to planting new churches. Conference leaders say they are waiting on denominational leaders to set a course for church planting. Yet conference leaders are not sure they want to be handed a predetermined strategy for planting churches that becomes the assumed model for all conferences. At the same time, denominational leaders observe that there is no orchestrated downward thrust for church planting from the denomination to conferences or congregations.

This is further underscored by an apparent internal conflict at the denominational level between the denominational mission agency's domestic ministries division and the denominational Executive Leadership office. As one mission agency staff member said, "Teams that were developed as part of the mission agency's [domestic] ministries department have been suspended pending further discussion with Executive Leadership regarding future structural alignment."

While the denomination and conference leaders attempt to determine proper protocol and structural alignment, participants in newly developing churches are confused about whom they should contact for direction and resources. Because of their regional proximity, conference staff members tend to be the first point of contact when the vision for a new church originates and when church planters are seeking direction. Conference leaders believe that they are best positioned to engage church planters and their key stakeholders by connecting them to resources for training and assisting in initial assessment of qualities and skills needed for church planting.

Second, the participants in this study all identified that the denomination and conference structures are not adequately prepared to engage visions for developing churches when these visions emerge from the grass roots. The four cases in this study are all examples of churches that have emerged even as the denomination's organizational culture and structural alignment are being defined.

The planting of Iglesia Menonita provides the starkest case of this lack of preparedness on the part of conference leaders. By the time the conference leaders were aware that a new church was under development, the church planter had already relocated halfway across the country to give leadership to that endeavor with the full expectation that he would receive financial help to do so from the regional conference. The leaders of the new monastic church plant, Hospitality House, a church that developed outside Mennonite Church USA, struggled to understand the procedures by which a developing church formalized its affiliation with the denomination. The church planter initially interpreted the undefined, two-year process that finally resulted in membership as the ambivalence of conference leaders toward welcoming a new congregation. All participants in this study agreed that the present method of church planting has been trial and error or "make it up as you go."

Third, leaders of new churches among ethnic minorities believe that the denomination and conference are not adequately prepared to provide culturally sensitive support and resources. There is a lack of culturally appropriate literature in the native languages of racial/ethnic church leaders. While it is unlikely that some of these groups are large enough to support the publications of such materials in the near future, the ability of denominational and conference leaders to become effective culture brokers becomes all the more important. Racial/ethnic church planters and their key stakeholders agree that there is limited understanding on the part of conference and denominational leaders with regard to how racial/ethnic congregations attain sustainability. This lack of preparedness results in a lack of trust, a sense of alienation, and a lack of sensitivity to the cultural assumptions with which racial/ethnic leaders necessarily contend within their communities.

If the Mennonite Church USA denominational system is not adequately prepared to meet the challenges of developing missional congregations of many cultures, it is in good company. The early church was not prepared for the Spirit-led witness in the first century either. Christians in Jerusalem were not prepared when the report came back of the conversion and baptism of Gentiles such as Cornelius (Acts 10:1–18) or the missionary impact rising out of Antioch in the commissioning of Paul and Barnabas (13:1–3). Suddenly the church was faced with a new wave of Gentile converts in Cyprus (13:4–12), Antioch of Pisidia (13:13–51), Iconium (14:1–8), and Lystra and Derbe (14:8–28).

Jewish Christians in Jerusalem were prepared to receive non-Jewish converts; the Jewish faith has a long history of welcoming proselytes into their religious community. However, they were not prepared to welcome converts who had no connection—in fact disregard for—the fundamental sign of belonging to the community: the tradition of circumcision (Acts 15:1–21). The Jerusalem community was willing to welcome new Christians into their space so long as the space remained "Jewish" Christian. For Jews and Gentiles to merge into a single body, the church needed to practice reciprocating hospitality that created a new space characterized by a select number of centered-set commitments.

Similarly, Mennonite Church USA leaders struggle to understand how to describe an ecclesiology independent of ethnocultural symbols. One of the four church-wide priorities is "global connections." Stronger connections to the global Mennonite community can provide an important platform to expose and correct tendencies toward ethnic ecclesiastical tribalism.

The issues of structural alignment at the denominational and conference level are complicated due, in part, to the basic assumptions that were carried into the new denomination from past paradigms. The lack of a clear path through the period of convergence in the change process resulted in a frustrated system.

One of the contributing issues appears to be one of organizational authority. A system in which it is not clear who is ultimately responsible for creating systemic alignment seems to indicate an inability to assign authority effectively. This may be due to the cultural predisposition of a dissident denomination that is suspicious of authority; the Mennonite church was born out of a felt need to protest ecclesial authority. There may be an organizational preference for avoiding the assignment of authority for the creation of systemic alignment. This was seen in one conference leader's comment: "I think there is something refreshing about each conference wrestling with 'How do we plant churches?' We are kind of on our own, but [I do not] want to be handed a plan."

The limited capacity within the denominational and conference structures to respond to the needs of racial/ethnic groups also contributes to the underperformance of the denomination. Currently, the Executive Leadership office has a half-time director of intercultural relations. One of the denomination's four church-wide priorities is "anti-racism." While a number of the denomination's agencies work at intercultural relations in mission, it is hard to imagine that staffing for this priority has been adequately allocated in the current configuration of Executive Leadership. Executive Leadership has indicated that if the growth trends of the denomination continue on their current trajectory, by 2020 half of all denominational members will be Spanish speaking.

Recently, denominational leaders have initiated plans to develop literature in Spanish. While this has been well received among Hispanic leaders and members, it has also become an occasion for leaders and members of other racial/ethnic groups to make stronger appeals for equal treatment. This has direct implications for the way denominational and conference leaders structure systems for resource acquisition and allocation.

Some Solutions

It is apparent, at the time data was collected, that the attempt to change the denomination's organizational culture and structure had become arrested. Further, the lack of alignment in basic assumptions, the inability to adapt to internal and external changes, multiple and often conflicting perceived realities, and a lack of internal integration of subsystems all contributed to the denomination's inability to realize the desired foundational ecclesial framework. This is at the heart of the Executive Board's declaration that the denomination's mission is not adequately supported by the current relationships, behavior, and organization.

Perhaps this is evidence of a postmodern understanding that organizational cultures cannot be controlled and changed by those in charge. Yet it does not seem helpful to decide that, because the culture of an organization has not experienced change, Mennonite Church USA leadership should not seek organizational alignment around an ecclesiology that is consistent with the denomination's most basic values.

Too many assumptions have not been aligned with the basic assumptions of the new paradigm. If, in postmodernity, organizational cultures are not to be controlled, it would seem that fostering productive dialogue that leads to generative learning will provide the best hope for organizational transformation. "If the organization is constructed from language" then "creating discourse within organizations offers more opportunities for organizing and thus for reorganizing—or change."[3]

---

3. Hatch, *Organizational Theory*, 368.

Hospitality House is a pathfinder for what preparedness for developing missional congregations might look like. This church has a very clear sense of missional identity seeking relevance in context. Its development process was "front-loaded" with clearly articulated, centered-set commitments. The words describing the centered-set commitments are an example of how language is socially constructing the self-understanding of the church as a unified organizational culture. These commitments differentiate the church from the world, yet articulate how it is engaged with the world.

Hospitality House leaders have developed an organizational culture that is aligned along the basic assumptions of *missio Dei*. There are various portals for entering the church's life. Persons new to the church community will choose the extent to which they will engage in the church's shared life while the standard—or "rule," or "center"—to which all in the church are being called is the same for everyone. This model demonstrates how a church can retain a clear sense of identity while giving itself over to reciprocating hospitality. It is possible that this model could be extrapolated to conference and denominational organizational culture and structures.

Overcoming lack of preparedness at denominational and conference levels is not a matter of developing a finely tuned church-planting factory that produces churches in cookie-cutter fashion. It is evident from this study that God is not waiting for the organization to become aligned before birthing new churches. This reflects the first-century pre-Christendom experience. Therefore, to develop missional congregations of many cultures, the denominational system may seek a structural model characterized by "receive and release" rather than "cause and effect." *Receiving* visions for developing churches would begin with a dialogue based on centered-set assumptions undergirding a missional ecclesiology. Where there is congruence in these basic assumptions, the denominational system would reflect the *release* of that vision to become incarnated in a way that can be *welcomed* in its context. This will require more attention to deploying missional understanding throughout the system and trusting that the essence of a missional congregation precedes its form.

QUESTION 2: THEOLOGICAL COMMITMENTS AND MISSIONAL ECCLESIOLOGY

At the heart of this book is an attempt to understand the nature of the churches that are being planted in one regional conference within Mennonite Church USA. Ecclesiology is the way we describe the nature of the church and, as such, ecclesiology is understood as "the most practical of all theologies."[4] Because the stated mission of Mennonite Church USA is to nurture and develop missional congregations of many cultures, it is appropriate to examine the theological and ecclesiological commitments present within the developing churches within Mennonite Church USA.

The second question in my study asked, "What common theological commitments are present in the churches being planted in one Midwestern regional conference of Mennonite Church USA and how are these developing churches aligned with a missional ecclesiology?" The interviews, documents, and observations gleaned from my study surfaced three sub-themes under the broad theme of theological and missional issues: (1) common theological commitments, (2) examples of positive missional reflection, and (3) examples of anti-missional reflection.

Common Theological Commitments

One denominational executive said that while Anabaptist theology seems to be a majority commitment among constituents of Mennonite Church USA, there may be some drift toward other theological streams. Interestingly, all participants in this study identified the theological commitments of the developing churches as being within an Anabaptist theological framework. In exploring the theological commitments of these developing churches, participants gave expression to a remarkably consistent set of core emphases. These emphases include believers baptism, the authority of Scripture, the normative teachings of Jesus, community discernment in discipleship, justice, peacemaking, reconciliation of all things as a sign of God's reign, simplicity in lifestyle, and an understanding of the church as engaged with but self-differentiated from society. In all cases, the way in which church planters and their key stakeholders talked about their aspirations and failures demonstrated a theological commitment to humility.

---

4. Ormerod, "Structure of Systemic Ecclesiology," 10.

Positive Missional Reflection

Interviews, documents, and observations gleaned evidence that an understanding of a missional ecclesiology is present to some extent among the participants in five ways. It will become evident that Anglo and racial/ethnic leaders differ in their perspective on how these commitments are expressed.

First, all participants expressed in some way a trinitarian understanding that God's mission to reconcile the world to God precedes human initiative in the context of ministry. This is the classic doctrine of *missio Dei*. All leaders in the cases of developing churches believed that their mode of "sentness" should be normative for all churches. In other words, none of the church planters or their key stakeholders expressed that the work they are doing is an aberrant form of ministry. While the church planters expressed a need for outside counsel and expressed gratitude for connection to a larger ecclesial system, they gave no indication that the work they are doing is in some way "on behalf of" a sending church.

Second, all participants expressed an understanding of the contextual sensitivity that is a mark of the missional church. The racial/ethnic church planters emphasized this contextual sensitivity in terms of the uniqueness of their own subculture within American society. The Anglo leaders and church planters emphasized cultural sensitivity, suggesting that anyone planting a church needs to spend time interpreting the context in which the church is being planted. A denominational leader suggested that this contextual sensitivity should seek to identify the polarities within a context in order to discover where the reconciling work of God in Jesus is occurring and, therefore, where the church's witness is most immediately needed. The leader of Hospitality House suggested that the need to interpret the context in which a church is being planted means that church planters should not do anything in the context until they have lived in the context long enough to be accepted by the residents of that context.

The attention given to context leads to a related third aspect of missional ecclesiology identified among the participants: hospitality. The missional church practices "hospitality by welcoming the stranger."[5] While this understanding of hospitality emphasizes the church's wel-

---

5. Barrett, *Treasure*, 169.

coming role, the participants in this study emphasized that hospitality, in a missional frame, is three-dimensional. The common life of missional churches reflects the reconciling hospitality of God, which has been given to believers as a gift of grace. Out of this awareness, the church extends hospitality to the world because the church has known the goodness of this gracious reception. But just as God allowed the world to set the terms under which God sent Jesus, the missional church's hospitality is formed by a prior sensitivity to the ways that the context is willing to host the witness of the developing congregation. Central to a missional understanding of hospitality is a conviction that God's love is never coercive in any of the three dimensions.

One denominational leader suggested that when planting a church, one wants to ask of the context, "Where would I be welcomed?" Hospitality House leaders suggested that the church's ministry can be understood only in the dialectic of hosting and being hosted. The pastor of New Covenant Hmong Mennonite Church became aware of the need to encourage his members to move beyond fellowship to the greater engagement with society involved in hospitality.

The missional understanding of contextualization leads to a fourth aspect of missional ecclesiology resident among the participants in this study: the intent to provide holistic ministry that seeks to incarnate the gospel story. Community Mennonite leaders suggested that the key to hospitality is looking for the places where the need for reconciliation and wholeness in the context most naturally intersects with the gifts within the congregation. Out of their common theological commitments, the leaders of these developing congregations and their key stakeholders are constantly asking how to develop a holistic ministry of reconciliation, peace, and justice that will model life under the reign of God.

Fifth, the church planters and their key stakeholders exemplify a missional ecclesiology in their reaction to modern expressions of the church as the steward and purveyor of normative social values. An indicator of the missional church is a church that "understands itself as different from the world because of its participation in the life, death, and resurrection of Jesus."[6]

Most of the participants in this study understand the church to be different from the world yet engaged with the world's need for reconciliation to God. They understand that the church is increasingly being

6. Ibid, 160.

moved to the margins of society and that its power will be derived from sources different from the world. For the racial/ethnic leaders, this can be understood in no other way. As ethnic leaders, church planters and their key stakeholders live in a society where they assume that others are privileged as part of the dominant Anglo culture. For Anglo leaders, this requires thoughtfulness. Anglo Christians have been socialized to assume a measure of privilege granted to them as members of the dominant power. A missional frame requires unlearning that assumption of privilege even as the church's power is being marginalized by society.

Anti-Missional Reflection

Three prior assumptions threaten to derail a missional ecclesiology.

First, denominational and conference leaders reported that rather than seeing the church as an alternative society, many constituents of Mennonite Church USA want the church to be a vendor of therapeutic services that will enhance the sense of well-being of the individual. One Mennonite leader offered this observation: "People want the church to help them live the life they have chosen a little bit better rather than asking the church to prepare them for life which is to come." This tendency forms churches toward a prior assumption of developing programs rather than incarnational ministries. If existing congregations attempt to develop new missional congregations, they need to understand how to avoid the tendency of the church to be a vendor of therapeutic services to prevent this tendency from being replicated in the spiritual DNA of the new churches.

Second, denominational and conference leaders questioned whether the members of Mennonite Church USA are able to participate in reciprocal hospitality. Just as the early church struggled to accommodate uncircumcised converts, it is easy for Mennonites to invite people into their space, as long as it remains "Mennonite space." It is much more difficult for Mennonites to imagine a reciprocal form of hospitality that results in the creation of a new space, even if, in essence, the new space embodies centered-set commitments.

There was a persistent but tacit hope, particularly among Anglo participants, that new Mennonite churches would feel like familiar, established Mennonite churches. In the case of Community Mennonite Church, longtime Mennonites who came to the developing church saw themselves as playing "host" to the "neo-Mennonites" who were founding the church. Among a number of participants in this study, there is an unspoken hope that developing missional churches of many cultures would result in churches of like-minded people who share certain ethnic patterns.

At the other end of the spectrum is the case of Hospitality House, whose emphasis on reciprocal hospitality was present from its inception. Reciprocal hospitality in this case is an explicit, foundational core value. Hospitality House has a remarkable ability to be present to its context, expecting little of the context other than making friendships.

In a follow-up conversation, the Hospitality House church planter shared a story that occurred as the church members prepared and served their weekly meal at a vacant lot during a major political party's national convention in their city. This meal consisted of wholesome food prepared on-site. On the eve of the major political party's national convention, the church members were going about this weekly act of hospitality.

As the meal began to attract guests of many nationalities, the scene was apparently "questionable" enough to attract a team of Homeland Security officials, who arrived asking investigative questions. Hospitality House members explained in theological terms what they were doing and promptly served up helpings of the meal to the Homeland Security officials, who received the food and remained in conversation with those gathered for the meal for the duration of the meal. This is a clear example of a church that is willing to extend hospitality by creating shared space with little fear that doing so will result in compromising the mission and convictions of the church. The willingness to immerse a church's life this deeply into a complex social context must be directly related to the security and confidence the members of a church have in their own centered-set core convictions. It is interesting to consider how bringing stories like this to the attention of the constituency of Mennonite Church USA might stimulate new experiments in other communities.

Third, because of the strong influence of nineteenth-century missionary models, leadership can often revert to replicating rather than recreating forms of church and ministry. In all cases, study participants tended either to borrow models of church and ministry from more programmatic approaches or to react to those models of church. In either case, there was a strong awareness of what other churches had done. Church leaders differed with regard to whether they were allured by replicating models of "successful growth" or repelled by the models that seem to "program" for the increase of numbers.

In any case, denominational and conference leaders and interviewees in three of the developing church cases struggled with the relationship between the essence and form of ministry in a missional frame. Again, Hospitality House is unique among the cases in this regard. It seems that at every level, the church planter and key stakeholders self-consciously articulated the way the essence of the church shapes the form of the church's ministry. Whether church leaders were allured by or repelled by the "growth" models, their responses are driven, at least in part, by the nature of the church-growth literature currently available and the lack of empirical research on developing missional churches.

One recent contribution to the empirical research on missional churches is the work of Lois Barrett who, with others, conducted case research on congregations thought to be missional. Her study identified twelve indicators of the missional church (see appendix B). Hospitality House is unique among the four cases in this study in exemplifying all twelve of these indicators.

Developing a missional ecclesiology as a foundational commitment within the organization culture will require the attention to leadership at every level. Interestingly, it would appear that congregational leaders within Mennonite Church USA have embraced a missional frame for leadership. There is, however, a gap between what pastors and congregational members perceive the role of the pastor to be. In his 2007 study of Mennonite Church USA, *Road Signs for the Journey*, Conrad Kanagy identified that church members continue to emphasize the "chaplaincy" role of pastors while pastors emphasize the role of "shaping the congregation's vision" and "equipping others for ministry."[7] This discrepancy in leadership expectations will need to be addressed if the grass roots of Mennonite Church USA will reflect a missional ecclesiology. In some cases, church planters are working in a context free of longstanding traditions. It is possible that the profiles of missional church planters can give established congregations the imagination needed to rethink what they are looking for from their leaders.

QUESTION 3: CONTEXTUAL PRESSURES

Missional ecclesiology assumes that missional church will be incarnational in essence but contextually relevant in form. The third research question in this study asked, "With what contextual pressures do church

---

7. Kanagy, *Road Signs*, 74.

planters and their key stakeholders contend in the process of planting churches?" The data from this study revealed considerable and weighty pressures that make church planting in the twenty-first century particularly difficult. The participants identified contextual pressures in two categories: cultural and social pressures and challenges to progress.

Cultural/Social Pressures

Denominational and conference leaders identified cultural and social pressures that broadly encompass those named by the church planters and their key stakeholders. These contextual pressures included a growing ambivalence toward organized religion in North American society, the marginalization of the church in society, inhospitable immigration policies, language barriers, overwhelming social complexity, and the pressure on Mennonites to acculturate into mainstream American individualism.

Not surprisingly, the most influential social and cultural pressures identified by racial/ethnic church planters and stakeholders involved issues related to their status as ethnic minorities. Broad social pressures with which these church planters and stakeholders contend include language barriers, inhospitable immigration policies, and poverty related to being displaced persons. Both Hispanic and Hmong church planters spoke of strong family pressure on those who decide to join a Mennonite church. In the Hispanic context, those joining a Mennonite church face family disapproval for leaving the Catholic Church. In the Hmong context, those becoming Christian of any sort face disapproval for leaving traditional animist religious practices, particularly as Hmong Christians eschew the services of the shaman.

The racial/ethnic church planters and stakeholders also identified a number of social pressures within the culture of Mennonite Church USA with which they contend. These forces include a perceived skepticism from Anglo churches, intercultural misunderstanding, and language barriers. Inconsistent patterns of offering financial support to racial/ethnic leaders contribute to the perception that Anglo leaders do not understand the unique contexts of racial/ethnic communities and the perception that racial/ethnic leaders are not to be trusted with the financial support they may receive.

Denominational and conference leaders characterized a key pressure that works against church planting as the desire for simplicity amid so much complexity. Church planters find themselves caught in the middle of competing values in postmodern society. This society values individualism, which assumes everyone wants to be left alone. Yet there is a hunger for community that will heal the individual's sense of isolation and alienation. Church planters struggle to represent the church as a place of hope, a place where questions can be asked and answers found. But many in this society prefer to see the church as a vendor of services offering simple solutions for coping with complexity. It is perhaps not surprising that these pressures were named by the Anglo church leaders and stakeholders, whose worldviews assume privilege. These contextual pressures are described from a Western worldview that assumes that the normative experience of Christendom is past. Among Anglo constituents of Mennonite Church USA, a primary commitment to the church can no longer be assumed.

Anglo church planters and key stakeholders described the attitudes present in their contexts as ambivalent toward organized and modern (Christendom) expressions of church. They described the people with whom they came in contact as preoccupied with busyness and inconsistent in the level to which they are willing to participate in the life of an organized church. While this ambivalence toward organized religion reflects the individualism of post-Christendom, church planters and key stakeholders also see in the people with whom they come in contact an intense search for belonging.

Challenges to Progress

The second category of contextual pressure with which church planters contend involves a wide range of issues that threaten to derail progress in developing missional congregations. Among denominational and conference leaders, these issues are matters of organizational and structural alignment. There is a perceived lack of clarity about who sets direction for church planting: the Executive Leadership office, the denominational mission agency, the conference ministry staff, or individuals with a heart for church planting. Denominational and conference leaders believe that there is more talk than action with regard to developing a strategy for developing missional congregations of many cultures. In the midst of this systemic confusion, church planters feel somewhat frustrated in knowing how to interface with the larger ecclesial system in order to find resources for support and training.

At a gathering for the church planters in this study, they were asked to identify what they needed most from their conference. The responses recorded in the proceedings indicate the felt need for more relational support and opportunities for learning. Church planters asked for strong, formalized, and living relationships between established conference churches and new churches; prayer and encouragement; leadership training opportunities; equipping for congregational leaders in new churches; and training in dealing with immigration/deportation issues.

Church planters and key stakeholders consistently identified the lack of financial resources as an obstacle to progress. Surprising to conference leaders, the church planters did not mention money one time in their joint gathering when asked what they needed most from the conference. This would indicate that while the lack of money is seen as an obstacle to a church's development, church planters do not necessarily expect that more money should be provided by conference or the denomination in the form of subsidy. Denominational and conference leaders and church planters all agreed that when church planters are bivocational, the distractions associated with outside employment slow down the church's development.

Though church planters and key stakeholders did not expect more financial resources to come from conference or denomination in the form of subsidy, it is unlikely that churches can be planted without financial resources coming from somewhere. It is possible that conference leaders, in their role of "making connections," could develop systems by which church planters appeal to nearby established congregations to develop partnerships for mission. These partnerships may carry the prospect of financial support for the developing congregation, but, more importantly, provide an opportunity for substantive relational exchange that creates a laboratory for mutual inquiry in the development of a missional ecclesiology. Conference and denominational leaders would need to give significant attention to how these relationships are structured to avoid the dynamic of what one conference leader has described as the relationship between a wise senior partner (the established congregation) and an ill-equipped junior partner (the developing congregation). Recovering the vision of "learning communities" as described in the denomination's formational document could provide the formative model for these relationships.

QUESTION 4: THE ROLE OF CHURCH PLANTER

A church planter is generally seen as the bearer of the vision for the new church. One denominational executive said, "As goes the vision of the church planter, so goes the church." The fourth and final question explored how church planters understand their primary contributions to developing the churches they are planting. Participants identified two key areas where the role of the church planter contributes to the development of a new church: the development of common understanding within the developing church, and leadership development.

Developing Common Understanding

Church planters are seen by themselves and others as playing a pivotal role in the development of common understanding about the vision and nature of the church that is being planted. With characteristic humility, the church planters interviewed for this study reflected on their *inabilities* to fill this role. It was often the stakeholders who affirmed the way church planters were successful in developing common understanding within the group.

Interviewing church planters on their role in developing common understanding in the church plant while sitting in the presence of key stakeholders provided the occasion for the church planters to reflect deeply in and on experience. Out of this reflection, the church planters expressed a desire to be less passive about articulating their vision. One church planter identified that separating his livelihood from church planting has made him a more effective and authentic leader. The church planters all expressed a desire to be more strategically prepared. They want to be more effective at transferring the vision to the members of the fledgling congregation. Though they want to be competent preachers and teachers, they feel they have few models for how to do these tasks in a context where the group is so small.

Leadership Development

Denominational and conference leaders believe that the denominational system may have a role to play in the leadership development of church planters. In the formational documents of Mennonite Church USA, framers envisioned an extensive network of learning communities for various mission initiatives within the new denomination. A set of learning communities was to be established for persons involved in church planting. A mission agency leader who was initially in charge of the learning community concept reported, "As far as I know, only one-time learning community events have occurred, none on a recurring schedule."

Church planters and conference leaders do not agree on the role that conference leaders will play in leadership development. Conference leaders expect that their role will not be to provide leadership training experiences but to connect church planters to leadership development resources. Conference leaders also believe that they can provide opportunities for quality control in the assessment of potential church planters. Church planters want conference leaders to provide leadership training experiences not only to church planters but also to lay leaders within fledgling congregations.

When church planters were asked about the role they play in leadership development, it is clear that they see this as one of their fundamental tasks. Key stakeholders were uniformly complimentary toward the role that the church planter had played in leadership development. The church planters were characterized as willing to share the platform. The church planters were concerned to provide leadership development grounded in the wisdom of the church versus the wisdom of the world. They also characterized leadership development as emergent based on volunteer initiative and felt need. The approach of the church planters to leadership training would best be characterized as constructivist, where the church planter is providing only the scaffolding necessary for the church member to reach the next level of competence. In all four cases of church planting, church planters agreed that the local congregation-in-context should be the center for theological training.

In the role of "making connections," it seems that conference leaders can provide the occasions for church planters to reflect in and on their experience by creating learning experiences that involve conference leaders, church planters, and key stakeholders. Absent any of these elements—church planter, conference staff, or key stakeholders—the story that is told may reflect a reality shaped to satisfy one of the participants in the conversation. Including all three players—church planter, conference staff, and key stakeholder—will ensure a level of vulnerability and honesty on the part of the participants that is a clearer reflection of reality and that will create a context for deeper learning and the development of common understanding. Including key stakeholders in the conversation between conference staff and church planter also draws the stakeholder into deeper reflection on the stakeholder's role in the developing congregation. This reflection would certainly provide the opportunity for key stakeholders to assess their role and competencies and to consider how they are contributing to or detracting from the forward movement of planting the church.

10

Findings and Recommendations

QUESTION 1

QUESTION 1 ASKED, "In what ways do the relationships, behaviors, and organization of Mennonite Church USA support or fail to support the development of 'missional congregations' within Mennonite Church USA and one regional Midwestern conference?" The interviews indicate that the relationships, behaviors, and organization of Mennonite Church USA do not yet adequately support the development of "missional congregations" within Mennonite Church USA. The attempt to establish a missional culture within the denominational organization has been subverted by an incoherent change process, resulting in growing structural misalignment in the denominational system.

How can denominational and conference leaders make progress toward the stated mission of the denomination? At the time of data collection, denominational and conference leaders seemed to be unclear about how to further develop the missional culture and bring structural alignment to the denominational system. Adopting a new missional paradigm as a basic understanding of the denomination's character and function has a direct implication for how leaders work at developing the organizational culture and bring structural alignment that will support a missional future.

The adoption of the new missional paradigm depends on how the parts of the church are aligned into a whole. At least three subcultures exist within the denominational system, each working with different levels of functional priorities. These subcultures include the executive culture, the interlocutor culture (regional conference ministry staffs), and the incarnational culture (those who are seeking to embody a missional ecclesiology at the grass roots). There are likely subcultures within each of these. Creating alignment among the parts of the denominational system "is not a case of deciding which one has the right point of view, but of creating enough mutual understanding between them to evolve solutions that will be understood and implemented," according to Edgar Schein.[1]

In declaring that the structures, behaviors, and relationships are not adequate to support a missional future, the Executive Board of Mennonite Church USA determined to manage the culture of the denomination by strengthening the control functions of the denominational executive staff by subordinating the other administrative structures and governance boards. Imposing an organizational culture through strengthened control is unlikely to produce a mature organizational culture in which the change to a missional paradigm can be anchored. This raises a fundamental question about the basic assumptions of the new mission paradigm for the denominational culture: does a missional ecclesiology itself offer a method for creating an organizational culture and structural alignment for the new denomination?

The basic assumptions of a missional ecclesiology call for analyzing the stories of the church in the context of a learning community seeking to understand what is going on from the perspective of mission. This approach examines narratives from those who are working to implement the "indigenization" and "pilgrim" principles, as described by Andrew Walls in *The Missionary Movement in Christian History*. If the presentation of the gospel is to be presented in terms that are relevant to a certain context, while challenging some basic assumptions of that context, analyzing the stories of the context and those who are working to embody the gospel in that context is essential. That is, how is the gospel incarnated in culturally relevant ways and how is the gospel *simultaneously* incarnated in ways that are challenging the context in which the church is emerging? The analysis of these stories explores how understandings of the gospel story are governing the development of new congregations in conscious and unconscious ways.

This story-based approach to developing a missional culture could carry the denomination to new levels of formative inquiry. The denominational and conference leaders would collect narratives of experiences of those who are developing missional congregations at the growing edges of the church. This approach to leadership could begin to align

---

1. Schein, *Three Cultures*, par. 49.

the denominational system around a *learning* function rather than an *instrumental* function, to the rich benefit of both established and developing Mennonite churches.

In this model, understanding develops in the organization from the particular to the universal, rather than from the boardroom to the grass roots. The learning organization enters that story, not for the purposes of troubleshooting and diagnosing problems, but for the purpose of constructing meaning. This form of dialogue is reflexive in nature. Reflexive dialogue requires those in the learning organization to suspend their assumptions to free the organization to understand the story as it is told by those who live it. In this form of dialogue, participants do not jockey to win the argument, but to collaborate in the construction of meaning. Reflexive dialogue becomes a core discipline of the organization, as leaders become "observers of their own thinking."[2]

We see an example of this sort of "meaning making" in the early church's struggle to adopt a new mission paradigm. Acts 15 recounts how early leaders met in Jerusalem to resolve the "pilgrim" and "indigenization" issues that emerged as the gospel spread beyond the Jewish community. In that remarkable event, space was opened for Peter, Paul, and Barnabas to tell the stories of how God was bringing reconciliation among Gentile believers. These stories challenged former assumptions about circumcision as a prerequisite for entrance into the Christian community. The stories that Peter, Paul, and Barnabas brought back from the missionary frontier not only challenged the prior understandings of the Jewish leaders, they also confronted the way former assumptions *weighed down* the faith experience of the traditional believers. These stories were received as an undeniable movement of God's Spirit (vv. 8–9). Peter said, "Now therefore why are you putting God to the test by placing on the neck of the disciples a yoke that neither our ancestors nor we have been able to bear? On the contrary, we believe that we will be saved through the grace of the Lord Jesus, just as they will" (vv. 10–11). This statement was the turning point in the debate that brought the whole assembly to silence and reflection (v. 12).

This story-based approach to constructing meaning also became the springboard for a dramatically repackaged understanding of the meaning of membership. The requirement of circumcision would no longer be imposed on the Gentile believers. James, the presider over the

---

2. Senge, *Fifth Discipline*, 242. Such a learning community paradigm was proposed by a missional transformation project conducted by the denominational mission agencies (Flaming et al., *Final Report*) but not implemented to date.

council, determined that "we should not trouble those Gentiles who are turning toward God, but we should write to them to abstain only from things polluted by idols and from fornication and from whatever has been strangled and from blood" (vv. 19–20).

Another way of thinking about this is by looking at the organization through a "symbolic" rather than a "political" frame, as described by Lee Bolman and Terrence Deal in *Reframing Organizations*. Instead of focusing on instrumental understandings that seek accountable results, leaders use "meaning" rather than "results" as the basis for organizational development. Denominational and conference leaders would view the system not in terms of the parts and output of a machine, but as a storied organism. The analysis of narratives collected "on the ground" would provide the indicators for what is needed from the executive and interlocutor subcultures. In other words, the analysis of these stories would surface how a missional ecclesiology is emerging from the grass roots and what kinds of resources are yet needed to further develop understanding in a missional frame.

A story-based approach to systemic alignment and the development of organizational culture is more consistent methodologically with a Mennonite theological framework *and* a missional ecclesiology. In short, a narrative approach to organizational issues helps Mennonite leaders be more Mennonite and those who want to be missional more missional in the development of mutual understanding for a common organizational culture.

The way of being for Mennonites is inherently story-based. There is no Mennonite identity apart from the text Mennonites read. Or as John Howard Yoder said, "The presence of the text within the community is an inseparable part of the community's act of being itself. It would be a denial of the community's being itself if it were to grant a need for an appeal beyond itself to some Archimedean point to justify it."[3] If Mennonite approaches to being and knowing are narrative, and if missional approaches to being and knowing are narrative, it only stands to reason that learning through stories will result in a more coherent organizational structure for a Mennonite missional culture.

QUESTION 2

Question 2 asked, "What common theological commitments are present in the churches being planted in one regional Midwestern conference of

---

3. Yoder, *To Hear the Word*, 114.

Mennonite Church USA, and how are these developing churches aligned with a missional ecclesiology?" The interviews indicate that there are significant common theological commitments among the church plants, and there is evidence that a missional ecclesiology is operational among the church planters and their key stakeholders. The church-planting cases demonstrate missional understandings resident among church planters and their key stakeholders. Additionally, this study surfaced a deepened understanding of three-dimensional hospitality as a foundational and formative missional value.

Two dimensions of hospitality are rather conventional: demonstrating hospitality in the common life of the church members and welcoming the stranger. Another dimension of hospitality precedes the other two and can easily be overlooked when churches are being planted: receiving the hospitality of those in the context in which a church is being planted. One church planter pled that this understanding of hospitality is foundational for all church planting: "Before you plant a church you need to submit to the neighborhood for a while first. So ideally, someone should just work and live and hang out in the neighborhood for at least a year before they even start doing anything tangible as far as ministry so they are really understanding where they are."

Interestingly, this understanding of hospitality was foundational to the missionary experiments Jesus conducted with his disciples (for example, Mark 6:7–13; Luke 9:1–6; 10:1–20). In all these cases, Jesus sent out the disciples with the mandate to receive the hospitality that anyone offered. Luke is most emphatic: "Whatever house you enter, first say, 'Peace to this house!' And if a person is there who shares in peace your peace will rest on that person; but if not, it will return to you. Remain in the same house eating and drinking whatever they provide, for the laborer deserves his wages. Do not move about from house to house" (Luke 10:5-7). When the disciples returned from this mission, they were bubbling with accounts of miraculous occurrences of healing and exor¬cism: "Lord, in your name even the demons submit to us!" (v. 17). This is the only place in the Gospels where we see a trinitarian response of ecstatic joy as Jesus, full of joy in the Holy Spirit, prays to the Father (vv. 21–24).

There is little in the research literature that emphasizes this aspect of hospitality. So much of the strategic analysis that is a part of preplanting planning is done from the vantage point of *diagnosing* the context rather than *being received by* the context. This is a place where denominational church-planting strategists could learn much from the stories of those who have worked diligently to apply the "indigenizing" and "pilgrim" principles in cross-cultural and international contexts.

The developing congregations in this study are contextualizing their ministries in communities where an awareness of Mennonite theology is not assumed. Because of their newness, their small size, and the incredible energy required in the startup of a new congregation, church plants often exist under the radar of the denomination. Yet these churches provide excellent case material for understanding how a missional ecclesiology emerges: they demonstrate the "pilgrim" and "indigenization" principles because, given their context, they must. They may do it better or worse, consistently or inconsistently. Nevertheless, they all must be working at the issue of how to incarnate the gospel in culturally relevant ways while simultaneously working to incarnate the gospel in ways that will challenge the context in which the new church is emerging. A story-based analysis of the experience of these churches can provide an influential learning opportunity for *all* congregations of Mennonite Church USA, and beyond.

Locating points of tension between positive missional reflection and anti-missional reflection resident among developing churches (see the Table below) provides denominational and conference leaders a frame of reference within which to develop initiatives intended to increase the positive missional understandings while decreasing the anti-missional understandings that threaten to derail the embodiment of the new paradigm.

The Tension Between Positive Missional and Anti-Missional Reflection

Positive Missional Reflection	Anti-Missional Reflection
The church as itself sent	The church as sending
Reproducing	Replicating
Church identifying the places of welcome in its context	Church hosting the context into the church's space
Incarnational ministry	Programmatic ministry
Church as engaged with but different from society	Church as the steward and purveyor of society's values
Church's witness at the nexus of contextual polarities	Ecclesiastical tribalism—the collection of like-minded people
Transformation	Colonization

Another issue raised in developing a mature missional ecclesiology has to do with a new wave of church leaders who are attracted to Mennonite theology through their reading and who are seeking a formal affiliation with the Mennonite church. This phenomenon creates opportunity for theological ferment as those who are embracing the church from outside the tradition interact with Mennonites who have grown up in the tradition but have read little theology.

One case of church planting in this study includes two founding couples joined by two couples who are lifelong Mennonites. The lifelong Mennonites labeled the founding couples "neo-Mennonites" and assumed a curious position of "hosting" the founding leaders of this developing church into the tradition. One wonders how the dynamics will develop between those who "know" the tradition by familial socialization and those who are "learning the tradition" through more intellectual reflection.

By adopting a story-based learning-community approach to developing a missional culture, denominational and conference leaders will create elevated platforms for "neo-Mennonites" to tell their stories of coming to the denomination so that they are not overwhelmed or frustrated by a culture in which the theological distinctives are largely assumed and seldom articulated. Hearing these stories, and the fresh articulation of Mennonite theology they embody, will also challenge lifelong Mennonites to deeper and more articulate reflection on their own theological commitments. At a time when many lifelong Mennonites are wandering away from the church for a variety of reasons, these stories could inspire those departing to think once again about the gifts this denomination offers.

This process could be further enhanced by collecting and analyzing stories from the growing sectors of the global Anabaptist/Mennonite family. The contemporary European context reflects post-Christendom reality more acutely than in America. Stories of people coming to embrace an Anabaptist or Mennonite expression in more acutely post-Christendom societies can provide opportunities for evaluating how issues of acculturation are at work in the same and different ways in an American context. On the other hand, stories from the Southern and Eastern Hemispheres of the global Anabaptist/Mennonite family, where the church is growing, can inspire U.S. Mennonites to reflect on the hope that the church represents in the face of environments that are often hostile to the church as an alternative society.

The interviews also show that there are a number of prior assumptions that threaten to derail the development of a missional ecclesiology. These assumptions include the desire among some constituents to see the church as a vendor of therapeutic services rather than an alternative society, the inability of some Mennonites to allow themselves to be hosted by others, and the tendency to replicate ministries rather than innovate reproducing, contextualized ministries.

All this offers significant handles to denominational and conference leaders with regard to development of a missional organizational culture. Though denominational leaders believe that Mennonite theology still holds sway among the majority of constituents, they are concerned that Mennonite churches are becoming less Mennonite in their theological orientation. Among the church plants, there is considerable consistency in theological commitments—commitments substantive enough to provide a core theology that can be the springboard toward a mature, church-wide missional ecclesiology.

QUESTION 3

Question 3 asked, "With what contextual pressures do church planters and their key stakeholders contend in the process of planting churches?" The interviews reveal significant and varied cultural and social pressures with which church planters and their key stakeholders contend as they plant churches. One constraining pressure all church planters named was financial constraints.

Other contextual and social pressures found include a growing ambivalence in the context toward organized religion, the marginalization of the church in society, inhospitable immigration policies, language barriers, overwhelming social complexity, and the uncritical acculturation of lifelong Mennonites into mainstream American individualism.

Obviously some of these pressures, such as language barriers and immigration policies, are felt more keenly among racial/ethnic church planters and stakeholders. Because one of the four church-wide priorities of Mennonite Church USA is to be an "anti-racist" denomination, considerable resources and time have been given to delivering anti-racism training to denominational, conference, and congregational leaders. Some in the denomination have complained that framing the priority in "anti" terms makes it very difficult to measure progress. Others contend that attempts to frame the priority in positive terms usually causes initiatives to devolve into generic multiculturalism. Those who provide anti-racist training remain committed to labeling the training "anti-racism" because of their conviction around issues of Anglo privilege that need to be deconstructed.

In the interviews with denominational and conference leaders, it was interesting to see the sensitivity that leaders felt toward issues of race within the denomination. When talking about race-sensitive issues, these leaders struggled mightily to find the words to express what they wanted to say. The anti-racism training seems to have deconstructed something among denominational and conference leaders. It may be time, at this level of the denominational system, to shift the attention from deconstructing racial prejudices to constructing common language with which leaders can speak more effectively to the issues. It also seems apparent from the data that the resources undergirding anti-racism training for leaders might be better allocated toward resources that could empower the church's prophetic voice to challenge inhospitable immigration policies and provide literature for leadership development and theological training in multiple languages written to specific cultures.

Church planters and key stakeholders need denominational and conference leaders to attend to the social pressures that are an inherent part of the overwhelming complexity of this current era. In highly complex social contexts in which paradoxical values are held together, denominational and conference leaders would do well to solicit from church planters and key stakeholders ways that they might provide leadership that doesn't further complicate progress. For example, because denominational executive leaders and the denominational mission agency's U.S. ministries department have not clarified who provides leadership for church planting, it becomes nearly impossible for church planters to connect to denominational resources, where they exist. The interviews show that conference leaders understand their most valuable role relative to church planters to be "providing connections." The denominational executive leaders of Mennonite Church USA would do well to provide more opportunities to conference leaders to learn the art of becoming effective interlocutors between denominational leaders and the grass roots.

Stories gleaned from church life in diverse and complex social contexts can provide important learning tools for all levels of the church to develop a missional culture. More than the mere collecting and disseminating of stories, stories must be accompanied with analysis that translates the underlying theological commitments that are at work in that particular context. Without this critical analysis, the stories will stand as shining examples waiting to be replicated by churches struggling to develop their own contextually appropriate missional perspective rather than serving as a springboard for innovation.

Returning to the issue of financial constraints with which developing congregations seem to universally contend, we see that the interviews reveal an important understanding about the role money can or should play in developing congregations. Money becomes a defining symbol both for the developing church's identity and for connection to the conference or denomination. When money has been collected from conference congregations and disbursed in the form of generalized subsidy from the conference to church plants, the church plants quickly identify themselves as a "project" of the conference, resulting in a growing dependency on the conference for sustainability.

Church planters were emphatic about their felt need for strong, formalized, and living relationships between established conference churches and new churches, prayer and encouragement, and leadership training opportunities. This is not to suggest that providing these needs would resolve the constraint posed by financial scarcity. Nevertheless, one wonders if the conference could explore developing a system in which money is given directly from established churches to developing churches. It is possible that this flow of funds would symbolize an investment that would result in relationships between established conference churches and new churches.

At the same time, naming the gifts that developing congregations might offer established congregations and developing systems for the deployment of those gifts would decrease the likelihood of creating dependency. It seems that the apostle Paul did not hesitate to bring the desperate need of the established church in Jerusalem to the attention of fledgling churches like that in Corinth (2 Cor 9). In this case, the need was monetary in order to respond to a famine. Today the most pressing needs of established churches have to do with more nonmaterial issues, such as recovering a first love, navigating the allure of acculturation, and learning how to bring "out of [the] treasure what is new and what is old" (Matt 13:52). The stories of developing churches working at the indigenizing and pilgrim principles are excellent ways to speak to these needs.

QUESTION 4

Question 4 asked, "How do church planters understand their primary contributions to developing the churches they are planting?" The interviews reveal that church planters understand their contribution to their churches as providing congregation-based theological education and leadership development. An unexpected but perhaps more substantial finding is the level to which church planters reflect in and on their experience and how formative this reflection is in the development of their own competency.

The way church planters understand the contribution they make to the churches they are planting has significant implications for how theological education and leadership development are done in the church. One key role that church planters play is to foster a common understanding with regard to the nature and vision of the church that is being planted. The interviewed church planters were clear that this is a *theological* task.

The other role that the data reveal is that of teacher and/or leadership developer. Because of financial and sometimes geographic constraints, participants in developing congregations often do not have access to formal theological and leadership development resources. This, however, was not perceived as a problem for one church planter in particular. This leader believed that his formal theological training has given him the capacity to do substantive theological training in his congregation. This is apparently the case.

Church planters believe that the congregation should be the primary center of theological education. Speaking of one of his members, one church planter said, "People wouldn't think he's not a seminary student and even though he's not gone to college or gotten any formal training of any sort, he's been saturated." This seems to be an exceptional example of a congregation as a theological and mission training center.

The experiences of church planters in theological education and leadership development raised fundamental questions that all in the church need to take seriously. A 2008 demographic study of Mennonite Church USA by Conrad Kanagy, *A Profile of Mennonite Church Planters*, identified that the top priorities church members have for the skill sets of their pastors are preaching sermons and providing pastoral counseling and care. The pastoral leadership role in a missional frame, however, is more akin to resident theologians focusing their best energies on teaching theology and leadership development. It would appear that the cases of church planting in this study are ahead of the trends in established churches.

Emphasizing the role of pastor as resident theologian in the congregation has implications for denominational and conference leaders as well as professional pastoral training programs. The church at all levels would benefit from the creation of new partnerships between denominational leaders and theological educators. Is it possible that denominational leaders working with seminary faculties could recover and implement the concept of learning communities for the sake of contextual theological reflection toward the development and implementation of a mature missional ecclesiology? Working together, these leaders could create rich and fertile opportunities for reflexive dialogue that would foster learning among leaders of established congregations, leaders of developing congregations, and conference and denominational leaders. The purpose of such events would be to foster a missional imagination at all levels of the church: the congregation, the denominational system, and the academy. In such learning communities, leaders can be better equipped as theology teachers in the congregation and become skilled in story-based approaches to interpreting their particular context of mission.

The richest and most moving segments of the interviews occurred when church planters were asked to reflect on their own experience. It became apparent that church planters operate at a capacity in which there is little time to step back and do this kind of reflection. Reflections in the interview provided significant opportunities for the church planters to discover fresh insights. In these processes, church planters found that they wanted to become less passive about articulating the vision for the new church. It provided the opportunity for one church planter to begin thinking about financial constraints in terms other than *obstacle*. He discovered his own conviction that having his livelihood separated from his leadership position made him a more effective and authentic leader.

The retreat for church planters was the first time in the conference's history in which church planters were invited to reflect on their experiences together. Because all expenses were paid and the church planters were reimbursed for lost wages, this event could be a priority for the planters. The evaluation conducted at the end of the retreat revealed that the participants experienced the event not only as educational but also as a validation of their roles as serious rather than quasi-church leaders. The church planters indicated that the corporate reflection that occurred was an important learning experience. Conference leaders present for the retreat said that they learned much as well.

These findings raise important questions about how the denomination and conference allocate their resources to support church planting. It may be that most of what church planters need to know about their task is already within and among them. Perhaps providing opportunities for reflecting in and on practice is one of the best resources conference leaders can provide—more useful and productive than formalized church-planting educational systems.

This hearkens back to a growing conviction connected to the findings of the first research question: a denominational missional culture should be structured around a *learning* function rather than an *instrumental* function where participants can become "observers of their own thinking."[4] To better equip church planters to develop common understanding within their developing congregation, denominational and conference leaders would do well to recover and implement the learning-community model that was conceived in Mennonite Church USA's denominational planning stages.

RECOMMENDATIONS

Structural and Organizational Issues

1. Executive Leadership of Mennonite Church USA should work toward developing a missional organizational culture and systemic alignment by implementing strategies that are congruent with a missional ecclesiology. Rather than imposing an instrumental approach to systemic alignment focusing on results, denominational leaders should seek to align the system around a story-based learning approach that is focused on the construction of meaning. The mode of such alignment will be generative learning, and the medium will be reflexive dialogue that considers how to leverage the strength and health of the organization rather than diagnostic discussion intended only to solve problems.

---

4. Senge, *Fifth Discipline*, 242.

2. Executive Leadership of Mennonite Church USA needs to effect greater alignment within the denominational system relative to church planting. Executive Leadership should be encouraged to determine what part of the denominational system provides leadership for the part of the denomination's mission that seeks to "develop missional congregations of many cultures." The development of new congregations in the twenty-first century may be more "emergent" than "strategic" in nature. Nevertheless, failing to attend to denominational organizational and structural alignment does not position Mennonite Church USA to fulfill its stated mission. The task of aligning the denominational system or developing missional congregations could be lodged in the office of denominational executive leaders, the denominational mission agency, or a consortium of conference-level staff. Wherever it is lodged, systemic alignment will likely not move forward unless Executive Leadership of the denomination determines the process by which that alignment will occur. Denominational executives should not wait on other parts of the system to align with the denomination's mission. This alignment will have direct implications for financial and human resource acquisition and allocation.

3. Denominational and conference leaders should recover the learning community model described in the formational documents of the Mission Transformation Project[5] as the core means of creating systemic alignment for a missional culture. To accomplish this task, leaders will need to be convinced of the value of a story-based approach to systemic alignment and educate themselves on the strategies that will foster such an approach. This approach will open important spaces for new expressions of the Mennonite church to elucidate the missional perspective the church seeks to embody.

4. Denominational and conference leaders should work together to determine a commonly held organizational understanding of how the denomination and conference relate to each other. Specifically related to the issue of church planting, denominational and conference leaders should articulate and formalize the leadership and services that each is best positioned to offer as well as where the responsibility for a system-wide strategy for church planting ultimately rests.

5. See Flaming et al., *Final Report*.

5. Denominational and conference leaders should determine processes and standards by which they are prepared to engage the vision for developing churches when that vision emerges at the grass roots. Prior to launching the development of a new congregation, significantly more dialogue is needed between denominational and/or conference leaders and those who wish to start new churches to explore the congruence of vision based on missional assumptions. Because churches become members of the denomination through membership in a regional conference, the systems of assessment for congruence of vision could also articulate a standardized process for becoming affiliated with a regional conference.

6. Denominational and conference leaders need to develop processes that will enhance their competency to deliver culturally sensitive support and resources. Though it is unlikely that native-language literature will be produced for all racial/ethnic groups, it is possible for denominational and conference leaders to develop better understanding of the populations with whom they work.

7. Seminary administrators and faculty are urged to be more alert to missional theology, to seek out more conversation with new Anglo and racial/ethnic Mennonite leaders, offering these leaders a greater voice in shaping Mennonite theological education.

Theological Commitments and Missional Ecclesiology

8. Denominational and conference leaders should leverage the considerable common theological commitments within the denominational system to develop strategies for increasing positive missional reflection and decreasing anti-missional reflection. One such strategy would include resurrecting the learning-community concept identified by the framers of the denomination.

9. Denominational and conference leaders should emphasize the biblical-theological significance of three-dimensional hospitality within the denomination. Collecting stories from situations of church planting domestically and internationally that speak to the issue of being hosted by a context could evoke imaginative learning for both developing and existing congregations in thinking about the nature of the church as sent rather than being a rooted institution.

10. Recognizing that the process of adopting a missional ecclesiology is also fundamentally an issue of spiritual formation, denominational and conference leaders should urge the church to pray for renewed understanding. Embodying a new missional witness will require nothing short of renewal in the church. The church will need to be led to new forms of hospitality and vocational prayer in which the daily prayers of the church ask God to reveal where God is at work and asking how the church might participate in that work by being hosted by those in its context.

Contextual Pressures

11. As they observe the emergence of post-Christendom realities, denominational leaders should inquire of global Anabaptists who have experienced these realities more acutely and learn how their theology, praxis, and educational programming have changed as a result.

12. Denominational and conference leaders should embrace the role of social commentator and become more effective interlocutors between the broad social context and those who are working in the grass roots. This will require developing greater competence and sensitivity in understanding how broad social forces are impacting different subcultures within the nation. By focusing on the tension of the "already" and the "not yet" understanding of missional thinking, denominational and conference leaders can investigate opportunities to enhance the positive missional reflection while decreasing anti-missional reflection among the constituents of Mennonite Church USA.

13. Where providing resources for church planting and mission are concerned, leaders at every level should embrace a preference for a culture of simplicity, without becoming simplistic, in seeking common ecclesial understanding in the midst of ever-growing complexity. Helping people navigate the complexities of twenty-first-century social realities is a ministry in itself.

14. Conference leaders should work at developing strong, formalized, and living relationships between established churches and new churches for the sake of prayer, support, and encouragement, as a context for ongoing leadership development and as a means of developing deeper missional understanding at all levels of the church.

Role of Church Planters

15. A denominational church-planting strategy for developing missional congregations should buttress the process of starting new churches with carefully articulated theological commitments couched in a missional frame. Carefully articulated centered-set convictions provide significant ballast in the face of a complex task. Centered-set convictions articulated from the start indicate that whatever level of commitment new participants bring, the call to faithfulness is the same for all.

16. Conference leaders can provide an immediate and significant resource for leadership development with church planters by validating reflection in and on practice as a core learning strategy for church planters. One-on-one and group experiences for the purposes of reflection in and on practice may be a more beneficial model for leadership development than formal educational programs such as church-planter "boot camps."

17. Denominational and conference leaders are encouraged to find ways of validating the two key roles that church planters play in their developing congregations: congregation-based theological education and leadership development. Further, validating the role of the church as a theological training center rather than a vendor of therapeutic services can be an important way to sharpen the understanding of missional ecclesiology within the congregation, conference, and denomination.

Afterword

THE STORIES THAT WERE opened to us in this book are rich beyond measure. They are stories of grassroots church organizers, stories of regional and national leaders who all want to participate in something miraculous in their world. They are stories of courageous people who imagine a new future in the midst of incredible complexity. What these leaders are seeking to do is bear witness to God's redemption of a world whose faulty foundations are crumbling before our very eyes. My hope in opening these stories to those who will read them is to illuminate the struggle to imagine a new world, the reign of God, which comes near when the gospel is embodied by those whom Jesus has sent to do so.

To tell these stories required an amazing level of humility and vulnerability on the part of those I interviewed. We should take that as an expression of an admirable desire for self-understanding and to do whatever is necessary to be better equipped to participate in the *missio Dei*. While the stories in this book at points reveal problems, lack of communication, structural dysfunction, racial insensitivity, and lack of understanding, everyone I encountered was crystal clear in their honest and steadfast desire to do something great in the power of the Holy Spirit.

A story-based approach to developing common understanding unapologetically moves from the particular to the universal. For in developing common understanding through the opening of these stories, we see a way of knowing that comes from the gospel itself. The kingdom of God, after all, is introduced into the world as a mustard seed that grows into a great tree where the birds of the air find a home; it is a small lump of leaven that when stirred into the dough makes the whole loaf rise.

May these collected stories, and many more, teach us how the kingdom of God has come near so that God's healing hope will flow through the church to the world.

Appendix A

Definitions

Anabaptism

The Anabaptist movement began in the early sixteenth century as a radical reform movement that challenged the established church's alignment with the state, the practice of infant baptism, and the exclusive authority of the church's hierarchy to interpret Scripture rightly. In contrast, Anabaptists practiced believers baptism, rejected violence, practiced discipleship in the way of Jesus, and emphasized communal discernment guided by the Holy Spirit in the interpretation of Scripture.

Contemporary convictions have been articulated for the global Anabaptist community, which includes a number of Mennonite denominations. Anabaptists affirm a trinitarian understanding of God, who seeks to restore a fallen humanity by calling people to fellowship, worship, service, and witness. Through the voluntary believers baptism, Anabaptists embrace the life and teachings of Jesus as normative for Christian discipleship. The praxis and worldview of the church are shaped by reading the Bible in community under the guidance of the Holy Spirit in light of Jesus' life, death, and resurrection. Empowered by the Spirit of Jesus, Anabaptists renounce all forms of coercive power, including violence, taking seriously the call of Jesus to love their enemies and work for justice for all. Anabaptists seek to live in the world without conforming to the powers of evil, striving to offer a holistic witness to God's grace through service, caring for creation, and inviting all people to new life in Jesus.[1]

---

1. See Mennonite World Conference, *Shared Convictions*.

Appendix A

Centered-set

A centered-set approach to belonging to a church is understood in contrast to a bounded-set approach. A bounded-set approach to church is determined by defining the outer edge of the community. The values of the community tend to be defined by the limits of inclusion. A centered-set approach defines the core values of the community that are at the center to which all are called regardless of how closely those relating to the community reflect these core values.

Christendom

Christendom generally refers to the historic period beginning when the church and state became co-extensive (ceased to be different from the society in which it existed) during the rules of Constantine and Theodosius. Christendom is more specifically defined in different ways, depending on whether the emphasis is on the church or the state. For Bryan Stone, Christendom refers to the conflation of the church and the state in "which the two are fused together for the sake of governance in such a way that Christianity becomes a project of the state or an appendage to the state, subject to its violent ends."[2] Alan Kreider defines Christendom as "a culture seeking to subject all areas of human experience to the Lordship of Christ."[3] Christendom in this understanding is characterized by common belief, common belonging, common behavior, and coercion.

Church plant

This label is given to a church that is under development in a new location. Church planting is the commonly understood term for beginning new churches. A working definition of church planting for the purposes of this book is "the activity of an individual, a group or the whole of an existing body of Christians aimed at establishing a new identifiable group."[4]

---

2. Stone, *Evangelism After Christendom*, 118.
3. Kreider, *Change of Conversion*, 91–92.
4. Bob Hopkins, quoted in Timmis et al., *Multiplying Churches*, 15.

Church planter

A church planter is the lead individual in the development of a new church. This designation is widely accepted as a class of church workers with a unique skill set that overlaps with general pastoral skills but includes specialization in the areas of evangelism, organizational development, and mission.

Contextualization

Contextualization is the process of communicating a concept or a construct into a given location in both verbal and nonverbal ways that make meaning among those in that place.

Discontinuous change

"Continuous change develops out of what has gone before and therefore can be expected, anticipated, and managed. . . . Discontinuous change is disruptive and unanticipated, it creates situations that challenge our assumptions."[5]

Generative learning

Generative learning is the process of becoming actively engaged with a situation for the purposes of developing personal and meaningful understanding. This form of learning is understood in contrast to problem-solving approaches to learning.

Key stakeholders

Most church planters develop new congregations in consultation or accountability with an ecclesial structure. These structures include parachurch organizations, regional and denominational leadership groups, and informal partnerships of congregations and/or individuals who provide some combination of oversight, support, and strategic discernment. In this book, the key stakeholders include a reference council, a ministry advisory committee, participants in the life of a fledgling congregation, and selected conference and denominational leaders.

---

5. Roxburgh and Romanuk, *Missional Leader*, 7.

Appendix A

Mennonite Church USA

The Mennonite church is "the thickest real-life embodiment of Anabaptist ideals and convictions."[6] Mennonite Church USA is a denomination born in 2001 through the merger of two historic Mennonite denominations. Missional theology/ecclesiology is the denomination's leading foundational commitment.

Missional theology and ecclesiology

Ecclesiology is a subdiscipline in theology. It is the study of the nature of the church. In the early stages of its development, the missional paradigm was referred to in the literature as a theology. It is increasingly applied to ecclesiology, the study of the nature of the church. Sometimes *missional* is simply applied as a modifier for the word *church*. Rather than seeing mission as one program of the church, the missional church is the community of God's people "who live with the conviction that [they] are a sent people (by our Triune God)—called to be a faithful sign, foretaste and herald of the kingdom of God. [They] are a people who engage in the task of bilingual theological reflection (recognizing the grammar of the dominant culture as well as the grammar of God) so that we can embody the good news in the context in which we find ourselves and join God in the renewal of all things."[7]

Regional conference

Mennonite Church USA has twenty-one regional conferences that exist for credentialing leaders, helping congregations in a regional area participate in mission that is beyond the capacity of individual congregations, and developing common theological understanding for faith and practice in the regional context.

---

6. Grimsrud, *Peace Theology*, par. 3.
7. Woodward, "Working Definition."

Appendix B

Twelve Indicators of the Missional Church

1. The missional church proclaims the gospel.
2. The missional church is a community where all members are involved in learning to become disciples of Jesus.
3. The Bible is normative in this church's life.
4. The church understands itself as different from the world because of its participation in the life, death, and resurrection of its Lord.
5. The church seeks to discern God's specific missional vocation for the entire community and for all its members.
6. A missional community is indicated by how Christians behave toward one another.
7. It is a community that practices reconciliation.
8. People within the community hold themselves accountable to one another in love.
9. The church practices hospitality.
10. Worship is the central act by which the community celebrates with joy and thanksgiving both God's presence and God's promised future.
11. This community has vital public witness.
12. There is a recognition that the church itself is an incomplete expression of the reign of God.[1]

---

1. From Barrett, *Treasure*, 160–61.

Author

David W. Boshart holds a PhD in Leadership Studies from Andrews University with an emphasis in missional ecclesiology. He is currently the Executive Conference Minister for Central Plains Mennonite Conference of Mennonite Church USA, with specific focus on witness and mission partnerships. He has pastored three Mennonite congregations in the United States. David is married to Shana, an ordained Mennonite minister, and they have three adults sons.

Bibliography

Ahonen, Tiina. "Antedating Missional Church: David Bosch's Views on the Missionary Nature of the Church and on the Missionary Structure of the Congregation." *Svensk Missionstidskrift* 92:4 (2004) 573–89.

Barrett, Lois. *Treasure in Clay Jars: Patterns in Missional Faithfulness.* Grand Rapids: Eerdmans, 2004.

―――. "Authentic Witness, Authentic Evangelism, Authentic Church." In *Evangelical, Ecumenical, and Anabaptist Missiologies in Conversation: Essays in Honor of Wilbert R. Shenk*, edited by J. Krabill, W. Sawatsky, and C. Van Engen. Maryknoll, NY: Orbis, 2006.

―――. (2008). *Response to Sheldon Sawatsky's Paper on Changing Mennonite Church USA's Behaviors, Organizations, and Structures.* Unpublished manuscript.

Bolman, Lee, and Terrence Deal. *Reframing Organizations: Artistry, Choice and Leadership.* 2nd ed. San Francisco: Jossey-Bass, 1997.

Bosch, David. *Transforming Mission: Paradigm Shifts in Theology of Mission.* 20th ed. Maryknoll, NY: Orbis, 1991.

Brunner, Emil. *The Word and the World.* London: SCM Press, 1931.

Buck, Stan. "Staying Power: Pastoral Tenure in 'Church Planting.'" PhD diss., Asbury

Collins, Lee, and Francis Hill. "A Descriptive and Analytical Model of Organizational Transformation." *The International Journal of Quality and Reliability Management* 17:9 (2000) 966–83.

Cowart, D. Keith. *The Role of Mentoring in the Preparation of Church Planters of Reproducing Churches.* PhD diss., Asbury Theological Seminary, 2002.

Davis, David. *The Evolving Role of the Founding Pastor.* PhD diss., Princeton Theological Seminary, 2002.

Eisner, Elliot. *The Enlightened Eye: Qualitative Inquiry and the Enhancement of Educational Practice.* Upper Saddle River, NJ: Prentice-Hall, 1998.

Finzel, Harris. "A Descriptive Model for Discerning Organizational Culture." PhD diss., Fuller Theological Seminary, 1989.

Flaming, Ron., et al. *Final Report on Vision, Strategy, and Organization of Mission Agencies for Mennonite Church Canada and Mennonite Church USA.* No. 11. Elkhart, IN: Mennonite Church Canada and Mennonite Church USA, 2000.

Flyvbjerg, Bent. "Five Misunderstandings About Case-Study Research." *Qualitative Inquiry* 12:2 (2006) 219–45.

Grimsrud, Ted. "Peace Theology." No date. Retrieved December 20, 2008. Online: http://peacetheology.net/anabaptist-convictions/3-from-sixteenth-century-anabaptism-to-mennonite-church-usa/

Guder, Darrell, ed. *Missional Church: A Vision for the Sending of the Church in North America.* Grand Rapids: Eerdmans, 1998.

———. *Missional Hermeneutics: The Missional Authority of Scripture: Interpreting Scripture as Missional Formation*. Mission Focus: Annual Review 15 (2007) 106–121, 125–41.

Hatch, Mary Jo. *Organizational Theory: Modern, Symbolic, and Postmodern Perspectives*. Oxford: Oxford University Press, 1997.

Hempelmann, Reinhard. "The Context of Christian Witness in the 21st Century." *International Review of Mission* 92:364 (2008) 45–55.

Hernandez, Rafael. "The Practice of Theological Reflection in the Supervision of Church Planters in a Multi-Ethnic/Cultural Setting." PhD diss., Andover Newton Theological School, 2004.

Hernandez, Twyla Kay. "A Missiological Response to the Emergent Latino Population in the United States." PhD diss., Southern Baptist Theological Seminary, 2005.

Herrington, Jim, Mike Bonem, and James Furr. *Leading Congregational Change: A Practical Guide for the Transformational Journey*. San Francisco: Jossey-Bass, 2000.

Hiebert, Paul. *Anthropological Reflections on Missiological Issues*. Grand Rapids: Baker, 1994.

Houser, Gordon. "Executive Board to Strengthen Vision." *The Mennonite* 11:4 (2008) 22.

Howells, Douglas. "Facing the Challenge of the Urban Frontier: Creating Effective Christian Church Congregations in the Cities of the United States." PhD diss., Asbury Theological Seminary, 2004.

Huebner, Harry. *Echoes of the Word: Theological Ethics as Rhetorical Practice*. Kitchener, Ontario: Pandora Press, 2005.

Jackson, Steve. "An Evaluation of Pastoral Self-Leadership and Church Health in Church Plants." PhD diss., Asbury Theological Seminary, 2005.

Kanagy, Conrad. *Road Signs for the Journey: A Profile of Mennonite Church USA*. Scottdale, PA: Herald Press, 2007.

———. *A Profile of Mennonite Church Planters*. Elkhart, IN: Mennonite Mission Network, 2008.

Keifert, Patrick. *We Are Here Now: A New Missional Era*. Eagle, ID: Allelon, 2007.

King, Jeffrey. "Creating Multi-Congregational Churches." PhD diss., Fuller Theological Seminary, 2001.

Kohlbry, Martin. "A Strategy and Design for 'Planting' New Churches Through the Development of Small Group Community." PhD diss., Fuller Theological Seminary, 1997.

Kotter, John. "What Leaders Really Do." *Harvard Business Review* 68(3), (1990) 103–111.

Kreider, Alan. "Beyond Bosch: The Early Church and the Christendom Shift." *International Bulletin of Missionary Research* 29:2 (2005) 59–68.

———. *The Change of Conversion and the Origin of Christendom*. Eugene, OR: Wipf & Stock, 2007.

Kreider, Alan, Eleanor Kreider, and Paul Widjaja. *A Culture of Peace: God's Vision for the Church*. Intercourse, PA: Good, 2005.

Lebo, Layne. "Identity Or Mission: Which Will Guide the Brethren in Christ into the Twenty-First Century?" PhD diss., Asbury Theological Seminary, 2001.

Manuel, Shant Henry. "Partnership in Mission." PhD diss., Acadia University, 2001.

McPhee, Art. The *Missio Dei* and the Transformation of the Church. *Vision: A Journal for Church and Theology* 2:2 (2001) 6–12.

Mennonite Church USA Executive Board. "Mennonite Church USA 2020: An Emerging and Future Church." February 4, 2006. Online: http://peace.mennolink.org/articles/purposestmt.html

Mennonite World Conference. "Shared Convictions." 2006. Retrieved December 18, 2008. Online: http://www.mwc-cmm.org/en/index.php?option=com_contentandtask=viewandid=4andItemid=7

Murray, Stuart. *Church Planting: Laying Foundations*. Scottdale, PA: Herald Press, 2000.

———. *Church After Christendom*. Waynesboro, GA: Pasternoster, 2005.

Nebel, Thomas. *Planting Churches in Small Towns and Rural Areas*. PhD diss., Fuller Theological Seminary, 2000.

Newbigin, Lesslie. *Trinitarian Doctrine for Today's Mission*. Edinburgh: Edinburgh House Press, 1963.

Ormerod, Neil. "The Structure of a Systematic Ecclesiology." *Theological Studies* 63:1 (2002) 3–9.

Palmer, Parker. *The Courage to Teach*. San Francisco: Jossey-Bass, 1998.

Payne, Jervis. "An Evaluation of the Systems Approach to North American Church Multiplication Movements of Robert E. Logan in Light of the Missiology of Roland Allen." PhD diss., Southern Baptist Theological Seminary, 2001.

Peachey, Paul. "New Ethical Possibility." *Interpretation* 19:1 (1965) 26–38.

Pierson, Paul. "Beyond Sodalities and Modalities: Organization for Mission in the Twenty-First Century." In *Evangelical,Eecumenical, and Anabaptist Missiologies in Conversation: Essays in Honor of Wilbert R. Shenk*, edited by J. Krabill, W. Sawatsky, and C. Van Engen. Maryknoll, NY: Orbis, 2006.

Rainey, Joel. "A Comparison of the Effectiveness of Selected Church Planting Models Measured By Conversion Growth and New Church Starts." PhD diss., Southern Baptist Theological Seminary, 2005.

Rasolondraibe, Peri. "Ecclesiology and Mission: A Lutheran Perspective." *International Review of Mission* 90:358 (2001) 331–37.

Roxburgh, Alex, and Fred Romanuk. *The Missional Leader: Equipping Your Church to Reach a Changing World*. San Francisco: Jossey-Bass, 2006.

Schein, Edgar. *Organizational Culture and Leadership*. San Francisco: Jossey-Bass, 1985.

———. *Organizational Learning: What Is New?* Unpublished manuscript, MIT Sloan School of Management, 1996. Online: http://www.solonline.org/res/wp/10012.html

———. "On Dialogue, Culture, and Organizational Learning." *Reflections* 4:4 (2003) 27–38.

Senge, Peter. *The Fifth Discipline*. 2nd ed. New York: Doubleday Dell, 2006.

Shenk, Wilbert. *Forging a Theology of Mission from an Anabaptist Perspective*. Mission Insight 13. Elkhart, IN: Mennonite Board of Missions, 2000.

———. "New Wineskins for New Wine: Toward a Post-Christendom Ecclesiology." *International Bulletin of Missionary Research* 29:2 (2005) 73–79.

———. *Forging a Theology of Mission from an Anabaptist perspective*. Elkhart, IN: Mennonite Board of Missions, 2000.

Sire, James. *Naming the Elephant: Worldview as a Concept*. Downers Grover, IL: InterVarsity Press, 2004.

Stetzer, Ed, and Connor, Phillip. *Church Plant Survivability and Health Study 2007*. Little Elm, TX: Center for Missional Leadership, 2007.

Stone, Bryan. *Evangelism After Christendom*. Grand Rapids: Brazos Press, 2007.

Thompson, J. Allen. "Church Planter Competencies As Perceived by Church Planters and Assessment Center Leaders: A Protestant North American Study." PhD diss., Trinity Evangelical Divinity School, 1995.

Tiessen, Douglas. "A Historical Ethnographic Document Analysis of an Invitational Partnership: A Case Study of the Evangelical Christian Missionary Union and the Christian and Missionary Alliance." PhD diss., Reformed Theological Seminary, 2004.

Timmis, Stephen, et al. *Multiplying Churches: Reaching Today's Communities Through Church Planting*. Ross-shire, Scotland: Christian Focus, 2000.

Turner, John. "A Strategy for Planting a Church in Northeast Cincinnati Using a Natural Church Development Paradigm." PhD diss., Fuller Theological Seminary, 2000.

Tushman, Michael, William Newman, and Elaine Romanelli. "Convergence and Upheaval: Managing the Unsteady Pace of Organizational Evolution." *California Management Review* 29:1 (1986) 29–44.

Tushman, Michael, and Charles O'Reilly III. "Ambidextrous Organizations: Managing Evolutionary and Revolutionary Change." *California Management Review* 38:4 (1996) 8–30.

Van Gelder, Craig. *A Theology of Mission and the Missional Church in the United States*. Luther Seminary, 2000. Online: http://cawley.typepad.com/A%20Theology%20of%20Mission%20%20The%20Missional%20Church.pdf

———. "Rethinking Denominations and Denominationalism in Light of the Missional Ecclesiology." *Word and World* 25:1 (2005) 23—33.

———. *The Missional Church in Context: Helping Congregations Develop Contextual Ministry*. Grand Rapids: Eerdmans, 2007.

Walls, Andrew. *The Missionary Movement in Christian History*. Maryknoll, NY: Orbis, 1996.

Wheatley, Margaret. "Turning to One Another: Simple Conversations to Restore Hope to the Future." *Journal of Quality and Participation* 24:3 (2001) 8–19.

Wickeri, Philip. "Mission from the Margins: The *Missio Dei* in the Crisis of World Christianity." *International Review of Mission* 93:369 (2004) 182–98.

Woodward, J. R. "A Working Definition of Missional Church." 2008. Retreived June 29, 2010. Online: http://jrwoodward.net/2008/04/a-working-definition-of-missional-church/

Yoder, John Howard. "The Theology of the Church's Mission." *Mennonite Life* 21:1 (1966) 30–33.

———. *To Hear the Word*. Eugene: Wipf & Stock, 2001.

Yukl, Gary. *Leadership in Organizations*. 6th ed. Upper Saddle River, NJ: Prentice Hall, 2005.

www.ingramcontent.com/pod-product-compliance
Lightning Source LLC
Chambersburg PA
CBHW050845160426
43192CB00011B/2160